THE EDUCATION OF CATHOLIC GIRLS

A Series of Papers by Nineteen Headmistresses
dealing with the History, Curricula, and Aims of
Public Secondary Schools for Girls

By

JANET ERSKINE STUART

With a Preface by Cardinal Bourne
Archbishop of Westminster

Originally published in 1911.

PREFACE

We have had many treatises on education in recent years; many regulations have been issued by Government Departments; enormous sums of money are contributed annually from private and public sources for the improvement and development of education. Are the results in any degree proportioned to all these repeated and accumulated efforts? It would not be easy to find one, with practical experience of education, ready to give an unhesitatingly affirmative answer. And the explanation of the disappointing result obtained is very largely to be found in the neglect of the training of the will and character, which is the foundation of all true education. The programmes of Government, the grants made if certain conditions are fulfilled, the recognition accorded to a school if it conforms to a certain type, these things may have raised the standard of teaching, and forced attention to subjects of learning which were neglected; they have done little to promote education in the real sense of the term. Nay, more than this, the insistence on certain types of instruction which they have compelled has in too many cases paralysed the efforts of teachers who in their hearts were striving after a better way.

The effect on some of our Catholic schools of the newer methods has not been free from harm. Compelled by force of circumstances, parental or financial, to throw themselves into the current of modern educational effort, they have at the same time been obliged to abandon the quieter traditional ways which, while making less display, left a deeper impress on the character of their pupils. Others have had the courage to cling closely to hallowed methods built up on the wisdom and experience of the past, and have united with them all that was not contradictory in recent educational requirements. They may, thereby, have seemed to some waiting in sympathy with the present, and attaching too great value to the past. The test of time will probably show that they have given to both past and present an equal share in their consideration.

It will certainly be of singular advantage to those who are engaged in the education of Catholic girls to have before them a treatise written by one who has had a long and intimate experience of the work of which she writes. Loyal in every word to the soundest traditions of Catholic education, the writer recognizes to the full that the world into which Catholic girls pass nowadays on leaving school is not the world of a hundred, or of fifty, or of even thirty years ago. But this recognition brings out, more clearly than anything else could do, the great and unchanging fact that the formation of heart and will and character is, and must be always, the very root of the education of a child; and it also shows forth the new fact that at no time has that formation been more needed than at the present day.
The pages of this book are well worthy of careful pondering and consideration, and they will be of special value both to parents and to teachers, for it is in their hands and in their united, and not opposing action, that the educational fate of the children lies.

But I trust that the thoughts set forth upon these pages will not escape either the eyes or the thoughts of those who are the public custodians and arbiters of education in this country. The State is daily becoming more jealous in its control of educational effort in England. Would that its wisdom were equal to its jealousy. We might then be delivered from the repeated attempts to hamper definite religious teaching in secondary schools, by the refusal of public aid where the intention to impart it is publicly announced; and from the discouragement continually arising from regulations evidently inspired by those who have no personal experience of the work to be accomplished, and who decline to seek information from those to whom such work is their very life. It cannot, surely, be for the good of our country that the stored-up experience of educational effort of every type should be disregarded in favour of rigid rules and programmes; or that zeal and devotion in the work of education are to be regarded as valueless unless they be associated with so-called undenominational religion. The Catholic Church in this and in every country has centuries of educational tradition in her keeping. She has no more ardent wish than to place it all most generously at the service of the commonwealth, and to take her place in every movement that will be to the real advantage of the children upon whom the future of the world depends. And we have just ground for complaint when the conditions on which alone our co-operation will be allowed are of such a character as to make it evident that we are not intended to have any real place in the education of our country. May this treatise so ably written be a source of guidance and encouragement to those who are giving their lives to the education of Catholic children, and at the same time do something to dispel the distrust and to overcome the hostility shown in high quarters towards every Catholic educational endeavour.

FRANCIS CARDINAL BOURNE, ARCHBISHOP OF WESTMINSTER.

CONTENTS

Pair though it be, to watch unclose The nestling
glories of a rose, Depth on rich depth, soft fold on
fold; Though fairer he it, to behold Stately and
sceptral lilies break To beauty, and to sweetness
wake: Yet fairer still, to see and sing, One fair thing
is, one matchless thing: Youth, in its perfect
blossoming. LIONEL JOHNSON.

INTRODUCTION
A book was published in the United States in 1910
with the title, EDUCATION: HOW OLD THE
NEW. A companion volume might be written with
a similar title, EDUCATION: HOW NEW THE
OLD, and it would only exhibit another aspect of
the same truth.

This does not pretend to be that possible companion
volume, but to present a point of view which owes
something both to old and new, and to make an
appeal for the education of Catholic girls to have its
distinguishing features recognized and freely
developed in view of ultimate rather than immediate
results.

CHAPTER I.

RELIGION.

"Oh! say not, dream not, heavenly notes To childish
ears are vain, That the young mind at random floats,
And cannot reach the strain.

"Dim or unheard, the words may fall. And yet the
Heaven-taught mind May learn the sacred air, and
all The harmony unwind." KEBLE.

The principal educational controversies of the
present day rage round the teaching of religion to
children, but they are more concerned with the right
to teach it than with what is taught, in fact none of
the combatants except the Catholic body seem to
have a clear notion of what they actually want to
teach, when the right has been secured. It is not the
controversy but the fruits of it that are here in
question, the echoes of battle and rumours of wars
serve to enhance the importance of the matter, the
duty of making it all worth while, and using to the
best advantage the opportunities which are secured
at the price of so many conflicts.

The duty is twofold, to God and to His children.
God, who entrusts to us their religious education,
has a right to be set before them as truly, as nobly,
as worthily as our capacity allows, as beautifully as
human language can convey the mysteries of faith,
with the quietness and confidence of those who
know and are not afraid, and filial pride in the
Christian inheritance which is ours. The child has a

right to learn the best that it can know of God, since
the happiness of its life, not only in eternity but
even in time, is bound up in that knowledge. Most
grievous wrong has been done, and is still done, to
children by well-meaning but misguided efforts to
"make them good" by dwelling on the vengeance
taken by God upon the wicked, on the possibilities
of wickedness in the youngest child. Their
impressionable minds are quite ready to take alarm,
they are so small, and every experience is so new;
there are so many great forces at work which can be
dimly guessed at, and to their vivid imaginations
who can say what may happen next? If the first
impressions of God conveyed to them are gloomy
and terrible, a shadow may be cast over the mind so
far-reaching that perhaps a whole lifetime may not
carry them beyond it. They hear of a sleepless Bye
that ever watches, to see them doing wrong, an Bye
from which they cannot escape. There is the Judge
of awful severity who admits no excuse, who
pursues with relentless perseverance to the very end
and whose resources for punishment are
inexhaustible. What wonder if a daring and defiant
spirit turns at last and stands at bay against the
resistless Avenger, and if in later years the practical
result is--"if we may not escape, let us try to forget,"
or the drifting of a whole life into indifference,
languor of will, and pessimism that border on
despair.

Parents could not bear to be so misrepresented to
their children, and what condemnation would be
sufficient for teachers who would turn the hearts of
children against their father, poisoning the very
springs of life. Yet this wrong is done to God. In

general, children taught by their own parents do not suffer so much from these misrepresentations of God, as those who have been left with servants and ignorant teachers, themselves warped by a wrong early training. Fathers and mothers must have within themselves too much intuition of the Fatherhood of God not to give another tone to their teaching, and probably it is from fathers and mothers, as they are in themselves symbols of God's almighty power and unmeasured love, that the first ideas of Him can best reach the minds of little children.

But it is rare that circumstances admit the continuance of this best instruction. For one reason or another children pass on to other teachers and, except for what can be given directly by the clergy, must depend on them for further religious instruction. This further teaching, covering, say, eight years of school life, ten to eighteen, falls more or less into two periods, one in which the essentials of Christian life and doctrine have to be learned, the other in which more direct preparation may be made for the warfare of faith which must be encountered when the years of school life are over. It is a great stewardship to be entrusted with the training of God's royal family of children, during these years on which their after life almost entirely depends, and "it is required among stewards that a man may be found faithful." For other branches of teaching it is more easy to ascertain that the necessary qualifications are not wanting, but in this the qualifications lie so deeply hidden between God and the conscience that they must often be taken for granted, and the responsibility lies all the more directly with the teacher who has to live the life, as well as to know the truth, and love both truth and life in order to make them loved. These are qualifications that are never attained, because they must always be in process of attainment, only one who is constantly growing in grace and love and knowledge can give the true appreciation of what that grace and love and knowledge are in their bearing on human life: to *be* rather than to *know* is therefore a primary qualification. Inseparably bound up with it is the thinking right thoughts concerning what is to be taught.

1. To have right thoughts of God. It would seem to be too obvious to need statement, yet experience shows that this fundamental necessity is not always secure, far from it. It is not often put into words, but traces may be found only too easily of foundations of religion laid in thoughts of God that are unworthy of our faith. Whence can they have come? Doubtless in great measure from the subtle spirit of Jansenism which spread so widely in its day and is so hard to outlive--from remains of the still darker spirit of Calvinism which hangs about convert teachers of a rigid school--from vehement and fervid spiritual writers, addressing themselves to the needs of other times--perhaps most of all from the old lie which was from the beginning, the deep mistrust of God which is the greatest triumph of His enemy. God is set forth as if He were encompassed with human limitations--the fiery imagery of the Old Testament pressed into the service of modern and western minds, until He is made to seem pitiless, revengeful, exacting, lying in wait to catch His creatures in fault, and awaiting them at death

with terrible surprises.

But this is not what the Church and the Gospels have to say about Him to the children of the kingdom. If we could put into words our highest ideals of all that is most lovely and lovable, beautiful, tender, gracious, liberal, strong, constant, patient, unwearying, add what we can, multiply it a million times, tire out our imagination beyond it, and then say that it is nothing to what He is, that it is the weakest expression of His goodness and beauty, we shall give a poor idea of God indeed, but at least, as far as it goes, it will be true, and it will lead to trustfulness and friendship, to a right attitude of mind, as child to father, and creature to Creator. We speak as we believe, there is an accent of sincerity that carries conviction if we speak of God as we believe, and if we believe truly, we shall speak of Him largely, trustfully, and happily, whether in the dogmas of our faith, or as we find His traces and glorious attributes in the world around us, as we consider the lilies of the field and the birds of the air, or as we track with reverent and unprecipitate following the line of His providential government in the history of the world.

The need of right thoughts of God is also deeply felt on the side of our relations to Him, and that especially in our democratic times when sovereignty is losing its meaning. There are free and easy ideas of God, as if man might criticize and question and call Him to account, and have his say on the doings of the Creator. It is not explanation or apology that answer these, but a right thought of God makes them impossible, and this right thought can only be given if we have it ourselves. The Fatherhood of God and the Sovereignty of God are foundations of belief which complete one another, and bear up all the superstructure of a child's understanding of Christian life.

2. Eight ideas of ourselves and of our destiny. It is a pity that evil instead of good is made a prominent feature of religious teaching. To be haunted by the thought of evil and the dread of losing our soul, as if it were a danger threatening us at every step, is not the most inspiring ideal of life; quiet, steady, unimaginative fear and watchfulness is harder to teach, but gives a stronger defence against sin than an ever present terror; while all that belongs to hope awakens a far more effective response to good. Some realization of our high destiny as heirs of heaven is the strongest hold that the average character can have to give steadiness in prosperity and courage in adversity. Chosen souls will rise higher than this, but if the average can reach so far as this they will do well.

3. Eight ideas of sin and evil. It is possible on the one hand to give such imperfect ideas of right and wrong that all is measured by the mere selfish standard of personal security. The frightened question about some childish wrong-doing--"is it a mortal sin?" often indicates that fear of punishment is the only aspect under which sin appears to the mind; while a satisfied tone in saying "it is only a venial sin" looks like a desire to see what liberties may be taken with God without involving too serious consequences to self. "It is wrong" ought to be enough, and the less children talk of mortal sin

the better--to talk of it, to discuss with them whether this or that is a mortal sin, accustoms them to the idea. When they know well the conditions which make a sin grave without illustrations by example which are likely to obscure the subject rather than clear it up, when their ideas of right and duty and obligation are clear, when "I ought" has a real meaning for them, we shall have a stronger type of character than that which is formed on detailed considerations of different degrees of guilt.

On the other hand it is possible to confuse and torment children by stories of the exquisite delicacy of the consciences of the saints, as St. Aloysius, setting before them a standard that is beyond their comprehension or their degree of grace, and making them miserable because they cannot conform to it.

It is a great safeguard against sin to realize that duty must be done, at any cost, and that Christianity means self-denial and taking up the cross.

4. Eight thoughts of the four last things. True thoughts of death are not hard for children to grasp, to their unspoiled faith it is a simple and joyful thing to go to God. Later on the dreary pageantry and the averted face of the world from that which is indeed its doom obscure the Christian idea, and the mind slips back to pagan grief, as if there were no life to come.

Eight thoughts of judgment are not so hard to give if the teaching is sincere and simple, free from exaggerations and phantoms of dread, and on the other hand clear from an incredulous protest against

God's holding man responsible for his acts.

But to give right thoughts of hell and heaven taxes the best resources of those who wish to lay foundations well, for they are to be foundations for life, and the two lessons belong together, corner-stones of the building, to stand in view as long as it shall stand and never to be forgotten.

The two lessons belong together as the final destiny of man, fixed by his own act, *this* or *that*. And they have to be taught with all the force and gravity and dignity which befits the subject, and in such a way that after years will find nothing to smile at and nothing to unlearn. They have to be taught as the mind of the present time can best apprehend them, not according to the portraiture of mediaeval pictures, but in a language perhaps not more true and adequate in itself but less boisterous and more comprehensible to our self-conscious and introspective moods. Father Faber's treatment of these last things, hell and heaven, would furnish matter for instruction not beyond the understanding of those in their last years at school, and of a kind which if understood must leave a mark upon the mind for life. [1 See Appendix I.]

5. Eight views of Jesus Christ and His mother. For Catholic children this relationship is not a thing far off, but the faith which teaches them of God Incarnate bids them also understand that He is their own "God who gives joy to their youth"--and that His mother is also theirs. There are many incomprehensible things in which children are taught to affirm their belief, and the acts of faith in

which they recite these truths are far beyond their understanding. But they can and do understand if we take pains to teach them that they are loved by Our Lord each one alone, intimately and personally, and asked to love in return. "Suffer the little children to come unto Me, and forbid them not," is not for them a distant echo of what was heard long ago in the Holy Land, it is no story, but a living reality of to day. They are themselves the children who are invited to come to Him, better off indeed than those first called, since they are not now rebuked or kept off by the Apostles but brought to the front and given the first places, invited by order of His Vicar from their earliest years to receive the Bread of Heaven, and giving delight to His representatives on earth by accepting the invitation.

It is the reality as contrasted with the story that is the prerogative of the Catholic child. Jesus and Mary are real, and are its own closest kin, all but visible, at moments intensely felt as present. They are there in joy and in trouble, when every one else fails in understanding or looks displeased there is this refuge, there is this love which always forgives, and sets things right, and to whom nothing is unimportant or without interest. Companionship in loneliness, comfort in trouble, relief in distress, endurance in pain are all to be found in them. With Jesus and Mary what is there in the whole world of which a Catholic child should be afraid. And this glorious strength of theirs made perfect in child-martyrs in many ages will make them again child-martyrs now if need be, or confessors of the holy faith as they are not seldom called upon, even now, to show themselves.

There is a strange indomitable courage in children which has its deep springs in these Divine things; the strength which they find in Holy Communion and in their love for Jesus and Mary is enough to overcome in them all weakness and fear.

6. Eight thoughts of the faith and practice of Christian life. And here it is necessary to guard against what is childish, visionary, and exuberant, against things that only feed the fancy or excite the imagination, against practices which are adapted to other races than ours, but with us are liable to become unreal and irreverent, against too vivid sense impressions and especially against attaching too much importance to them, against grotesque and puerile forms of piety, which drag down the beautiful devotions to the saints until they are treated as inhabitants of a superior kind of doll's house, rewarded and punished, scolded and praised, endowed with pet names, and treated so as to become objects of ridicule to those who do not realize that these extravagances may be in other countries natural forms of peasant piety when the grace of intimacy with the saints has run wild. In northern countries a greater sobriety of devotion is required if it is to have any permanent influence on life.

But again, on the other hand, the more restrained devotion must not lose its spontaneity; so long as it is the true expression of faith it can hardly be too simple, it can never be too intimate a part of common life. Noble friendships with the saints in glory are one of the most effectual means of learning heavenly-mindedness, and friendships formed in childhood will last through a lifetime. To find a character like one's own which has fought the same fight and been crowned, is an encouragement which obtains great victories, and to enter into the thoughts of the saints is to qualify oneself here below for intercourse with the citizens of heaven.

To be well grounded in the elements of faith, and to have been so taught that the practice of religion has become the atmosphere of a happy life, to have the habit of sanctifying daily duties, joys, and trials by the thought of God, and a firm resolve that nothing shall be allowed to draw the soul away from Him, such is, broadly speaking, the aim we may set before ourselves for the end of the years of childhood, after which must follow the more difficult years of the training of youth.

The time has gone by when the faith of childhood might be carried through life and be assailed by no questionings from without. A faith that is not armed and ready for conflict stands a poor chance of passing victoriously through its trials, it cannot hope to escape from being tried. "We have laboured successfully," wrote a leading Jewish Freemason in Rome addressing his Brotherhood, "in the great cities and among the young men; it remains for us to carry out the work in the country districts and amongst the women." Words could not be plainer to show what awaits the faith of children when they come out into the world; and even in countries where the aim is not so clearly set forth the current of opinion mostly sets against the faith, the current of the world invariably does so. For faith to hold on its course against all that tends to carry it away, it is needful that it should not be found unprepared. The minds of the young cannot expect to be carried along by a Catholic public opinion, there will be few to help them, and they must learn to stand by themselves, to answer for themselves, to be challenged and not afraid to speak out for their faith, to be able to give "first aid" to unsettled minds and not allow their own to be unsettled by what they hear. They must learn that, as Father Dalgairns points out, their position in the world is far more akin to that of Christians in the first centuries of the Church than to the life that was lived in the middle ages when the Church visibly ruled over public opinion. Now, as in the earliest ages, the faithful stand in small assemblies or as individuals amid cold or hostile surroundings, and individual faith and sanctity are the chief means of extending the kingdom of God on earth.

But this apostleship needs preparation and training. The early teaching requires to be seasoned and hardened to withstand the influences which tend to dissolve faith and piety; by this seasoning faith must be enlightened, and piety become serene and grave, "sedate," as St. Francis of Sales would say with beautiful commentary. In the last years of school or school-room life the mind has to be gradually inured to the harder life, to the duty of defending as well as adorning the faith, and to gain at least some idea of the enemies against which defence must be made. It is something even to know what is in the air and what may be expected that the first surprise may not disturb the balance of the mind. To know that in the Church there have been sorrows and scandals, without the promises of

Christ having failed, and even that it had to be so,
fulfilling His word, "it must needs be that scandals
come" (St. Matthew XVIII. 7), that they are
therefore rather a confirmation than a stumbling-
block to our faith, this is a necessary safeguard. To
have some unpretentious knowledge of what is said
and thought concerning Holy Scripture, to know at
least something about Modernism and other phases
of current opinion is necessary, without making a
study of their subtilties, for the most insecure
attitude of mind for girls is to *think they know*, in
these difficult questions, and the best safeguard
both of their faith and good sense is intellectual
modesty. Without making acquaintance in detail
with the phenomena of spiritualism and kindred arts
or sciences, it is needful to know in a plain and
general way why they are forbidden by the Church,
and also to know how those who have lost their
balance and peace of mind in these pursuits would
willingly draw back, but find it next to impossible
to free themselves from the servitude in which they
are entangled. It is hard for some minds to resist the
restless temptation to feel, to see, to test and handle
all that life can offer of strange and mysterious
experiences, and next to the curb of duty comes the
safeguard of greatly valuing freedom of mind.

Curiosity concerning evil or dangerous knowledge
is more impetuous when a sudden emancipation of
mind sweeps the old landmarks and restraints out of
sight, and nothing has been foreseen which can
serve as a guide. Then is the time when weak places
in education show themselves, when the least
insincerity in the presentment of truth brings its
own punishment, and a faith not pillared and

grounded in all honesty is in danger of failing. The best security is to have nothing to unlearn, to know that what one knows is a very small part of what can be known, but that as far as it goes it is true and genuine, and cannot be outgrown, that it will stand both the wear of time and the test of growing power of thought, and that those who have taught these beliefs will never have to retract or be ashamed of them, or own that they were passed off, though inadequate, upon the minds of children.

It is not unusual to meet girls who are troubled with "doubts" as to faith and difficulties which alarm both them and their friends. Sometimes when these "doubts" are put into words they turn out to be mere difficulties, and it has not been understood that "ten thousand difficulties do not make a doubt." Sometimes the difficulties are scarcely real, and come simply from catching up objections which they do not know how to answer, and think unanswerable. Sometimes a spirit of contradiction has been aroused, and a captious tendency, or a love of excitement and sensationalism, with a wish to see the other side. Sometimes imperfect teaching has led them to expect the realization of things as seen, which are only to be assented to as believed, so that there is a hopeless effort to *imagine*, to *feel*, and to *feel sure*, to lean in some way upon what the senses can verify, and the acquiescence, assent, and assurance of faith seems all insufficient to give security. Sometimes there is genuine ignorance of what is to be believed, and of what it is to believe. Sometimes it is merely a question of nerves, a want of tone in the mind, insufficient occupation and training which has thrown the mind back upon itself

to its own confusion. Sometimes they come from
want of understanding that there must be mysteries
in faith, and a multitude of questions that do not
admit of complete answers, that God would not be
God if the measure of our minds could compass
His, that the course of His Providence must
transcend our experience and judgment, and that if
the truths of faith forced the assent of our minds all
the value of that assent would be taken away. If
these causes and a few others were removed one
may ask oneself how many "doubts" and difficulties
would remain in the ordinary walks of Catholic life.

It seems to be according to the mind of the Church
in our days to turn the minds of her children to the
devotional study of Scripture, and if this is begun,
as it may be, in the early years of education it gains
an influence which is astonishing. The charm of the
narrative in the very words of Scripture, and the
jewels of prayer and devotion which may be
gathered in the Sacred Books, are within the reach
of children, and they prepare a treasure of
knowledge and love which will grow in value
during a lifetime. Arms are there, too, against many
difficulties and temptations; and a better
understanding of the Church's teaching and of the
liturgy which is the best standard of devotion for the
faithful.

The blight of Scriptural knowledge is to make it a
"subject" for examinations, running in a parallel
track with Algebra and Geography, earning its
measure of marks and submitted to the tests of non-
Catholic examining bodies, to whom it speaks in
another tongue than ours. It must be a very robust

devotion to the word of God that is not chilled by such treatment, and can keep an early Christian glow in its readings of the Gospels and Epistles whether they have proved a failure or a success in the examination. In general, Catholic candidates acquit themselves well in this subject, and perhaps it may give some edification to non-Catholic examiners when they see these results. But it is questionable whether the risk of drying up the affection of children for what must become to them a text-book is worth this measure of success. Let experience speak for those who know if it is not so; it would seem in the nature of things that so it must be. When it is given over to voluntary study (beyond the diocesan requirements which are a stimulus and not a blight) it catches, not like wild fire, but like blessed fire, even among young children, and is woven imperceptibly into the texture of life.

Lastly, what may be asked of Catholic children when they grow up and have to take upon themselves the responsibility of keeping their own faith alive, and the practice of their religion in an atmosphere which may often be one of cold faith and slack observance? Neither their spiritual guides, nor those who have educated them, nor their own parents, can take this responsibility out of their hands. St. Francis of Sales calls science the 8th Sacrament for a priest, urging the clergy to give themselves earnestly to study, and he says that great troubles have come upon us because the sacred ark of knowledge was found in other hands than those of the Levites. Leo XIII wrote in one of his great encyclicals that "Every minister of holy religion must bring to the struggle the full energy of his mind and all his power of endurance." What about the laity? We cannot leave all the battle to the clergy; they cannot defend and instruct and carry us into the kingdom of heaven in spite of ourselves; their labours call for response and correspondence. What about those who are now leaving childhood behind and will be in the front ranks of the coming generation? Their influence will make or unmake the religion of their homes, and what they will be for the whole of their life will depend very much upon how they take their first independent stand.

It is much that they should be well grounded in those elements of doctrine which they can learn in their school-days. It is much more if they carry out with them a living interest in the subject and care to watch the current of the Church's thought in the encyclicals that are addressed to the faithful, the pastorals of Bishops, the works of Catholic writers which, are more and more within the reach of all, in the great events of the Church's life, and in the talk of those who are able to speak from first-hand knowledge and experience. It is most of all fundamental that they should have an attitude of mind that is worthy of their faith; one that is not nervous or apologetic for the Church, not anxious about the Pope lest he should "interfere too much," nor frightened of what the world may say. They should have an unperturbed conviction that the Church will have the last word in any controversy, and that she has nothing to be alarmed at, though all the battalions of newest thought should be set in array against her; they should be lovingly proud of the Church, and keep their belief in her at all times joyous, assured, and unafraid.

Theology is not for them, neither required nor obtainable, though some have been found enterprising enough to undertake to read the *Summa*, and naive enough to suppose that they would be theologians at the end of it, and even at the outset ready to exchange ideas with Doctors of Divinity on efficacious grace, and to have "views" on the authorship of the Sacred Writings. Such aspirations either come to an untimely end by an awakening sense of proportion, or remain as monuments to the efforts of those "less wise," or in some unfortunate cases the mind loses its balance and is led into error.

"Thirsting to be more than mortal, I was even less than clay."

Let us, if we can, keep the bolder spirits on the level of what is congruous, where the wealth that is within their reach will not be exhausted in their lifetime, and where they may excel without offence and without inviting either condemnation or ridicule. The sense of fitness is a saving instinct in this as in 1 every other department of life. When it is present, first principles come home like intuitions to the mind, where it is absent they seem to take no hold at all, and the understanding that should supply for the right instinct makes slow and laborious way if it ever enters at all.

To know the relation in which one stands to any department of knowledge is, in that department, "the beginning of wisdom". The great Christian

Basilicas furnish a parallel in the material order.
They are the house of God and the home and
possession of every member of the Church militant
without distinction of age or rank or learning. But
they are not the same to each. Every one brings his
own understanding and faith and insight, and the
great Church is to him what he has capacity to
understand and to receive. The great majority of
worshippers could not draw a fine of the plans or
expound a law of the construction, or set a stone in
its place, yet the whole of it is theirs and for them,
and their reverent awe, even if they have no further
understanding, adds a spiritual grace and a fuller
dignity to the whole. The child, the beggar, the
pilgrim, the penitent, the lowly servants and
custodians of the temple, the clergy, the venerable
choir, the highest authorities from whom come the
order and regulation of the ceremonies, all have
their parts, all stand in their special relations
harmoniously sharing in different degrees in what is
for all. Even those long since departed, architects
and builders and donors, are not cut off from it,
their works follow them, and their memory lives in
the beauty which stands as a memorial to their great
ideals. It is all theirs, it is all ours, it is all God's.
And so of the great basilica of theology, built up
and ever in course of building; it is for all--but for
each according to his needs---for their use, for their
instruction, to surround and direct their worship, to
be a security and defence to their souls, a great
Church in which the spirit is raised heavenwards in
proportion to the faith and submission with which it
bows down in adoration before the throne of God.

CHAPTER II.

CHARACTER I.

"La vertu maitresse d'aujourd'hui est la spontaneite resolue, reglee par les principes interieurs et les disciplines volontairement acceptees."--Y. LE QUERDEC.

The value set on character, even if the appreciation goes no further than words, has increased very markedly within the last few years, and in reaction against an exclusively mental training we hear louder and louder the plea for the formation and training of character.

Primarily the word *character* signifies a distinctive mark, cut, engraved, or stamped upon a substance, and by analogy, this is likewise character in the sense in which it concerns education. A "man of character" is one in whom acquired qualities, orderly and consistent, stand out on the background of natural temperament, as the result of training and especially of self-discipline, and therefore stamped or engraved upon something receptive which was prepared for them. This something receptive is the natural temperament, a basis more or less apt to receive what training and habit may bring to bear upon it. The sum of acquired habits tells upon the temperament, and together with it produce or establish character, as the arms engraved upon the stone constitute the seal.

If habits are not acquired by training, and instead of

them temperament alone has been allowed to have its way in the years of growth, the seal bears no arms engraven on it, and the result is want of character, or a weak character, without distinctive mark, showing itself in the various situations of life inconsistent, variable, unequal to strain, acting on the impulse, good or bad, of the moment; its fitful strength in moods of obstinacy or self-will showing that it lacks the higher qualities of rational discernment and self-control.

"Character is shown by susceptibility to motive," says a modern American, turning with true American instinct to the practical side in which he has made experiences, and it is evidently one of the readiest ways of approaching the study of any individual character, to make sure of the motives which awaken response. But the result of habit and temperament working together shows itself in every form of spontaneous activity as well as in response to external stimulus. Character may be studied in tastes and sympathies, in the manner of treating with one's fellow creatures, of confronting various "situations" in life, in the ideals aimed at, in the estimate of success or failure, in the relative importance attached to things, in the choice of friends and the ultimate fate of friendships, in what is expected and taken for granted, as in what is habitually ignored, in the instinctive attitude towards law and authority, towards custom and tradition, towards order and progress.

Character, then, may stand for the sum of the qualities which go to make one to be *thus*, and not otherwise; but the basis which underlies and constantly reasserts itself is temperament. It makes people angry to say this, if they are determined to be so completely masters of their way in life that nothing but reason, in the natural order, shall be their guide; but though heroism of soul has overcome the greatest drawbacks of an unfortunate physical organization, these cases are rare, and in general it must be taken into account to such an extent that the battle against difficulties of temperament is the battle of a lifetime. There are certain broad divisions which although they cannot pretend to rest upon scientific principles yet appeal constantly to experience, and often serve as practical guides to forecast the lines on which particular characters may be developed. There is a very striking division into assenting and dissenting temperaments, children of *yes* and children of _no_; a division which declares itself very early and is maintained all along the lines of early development, in mind and will and taste and manner, in every phase of activity. And though time and training and the schooling of life may modify its expression, yet below the surface it would seem only to accentuate itself, as the features of character become more marked with advancing years. Where it touches the religious disposition one would say that some were born with the minds of Catholics and, others of Nonconformists, representing respectively centripetal and centrifugal tendencies of mind; the first apt to see harmony and order, to realize the tenth of things that must be as they are, the second born to be in opposition and with great labour subduing themselves into conformity. They are precious aids in the service of the Church as controversialists when enlisted on the right side, for controversy is their element. But for positive doctrine, for keen appreciation, for persuasive action on the wills of others, they are at a disadvantage, at all events in England, where logic does not enter into the national religious system, and the mind is apt to resent conviction as if it were a kind of coercion. There are a great number of such born Nonconformists in England, and when either the grace of Catholic education or of conversion has been granted to them, it is interesting to watch the efforts to subdue and attune themselves to submission and to faith. Sometimes the Nonconformist temperament is the greatest of safeguards, where a Catholic child is obliged to stand alone amongst uncongenial surroundings, then it defends itself doggedly, splendidly, and comes out after years in a Protestant school quite untouched in its faith and much strengthened in militant Christianity. These are cheerful instances of its development, and its advantages; they would suggest that some external opposition or friction is necessary for such temperaments that their fighting instinct may be directed against the common enemy, and not tend to arouse controversies and discussions in its own ranks or within itself. In less happy cases the instinct of opposition is a cause of endless trouble, friction in family life, difficulty in working with others, "alarums, excursions" on all sides, and worse, the get attitude of distrust towards authority, which undermines the foundations of faith and prepares the mind to break away from control, to pass from instinctive opposition to antagonism, from antagonism to contempt, from contempt to rebellion and revolt. Arrogance of mind, irreverence, self-idolatry, blindness, follow in their course, and the whole nature loses its balance and becomes through pride a pitiful wreck.

The assenting mind has its own possibilities for good and evil, more human than those of Nonconformity, for "pride was not made for men" (Ecclus. x 22), less liable to great catastrophes, and in general better adapted for all that belongs to the service of God and man. It is a happy endowment, and the happiness of others is closely bound up with its own. Again, its faults being more human are more easily corrected, and fortunately for the possessor, punish themselves more often. This favours truthfulness in the mind and humility in the soul--the spirit of the *Confiteor*. Its dangers are those of too easy assent, of inordinate pursuit of particular good, of inconstancy and variability, of all the humanistic elements which lead back to paganism. The history of the Renaissance in Southern Europe testifies to this, as it illustrates in other countries the development of the spirit of Nonconformity and revolt. Calvinism and a whole group of Protestant schools of thought may stand as examples of the spirit of denial working itself out to its natural consequences; while the exaggerations of Italian humanism, frankly pagan, are fair illustrations of the spirit of assent carried beyond bounds. And those centuries when the tide of life ran high for good or evil, furnish instances in point abounding with interest and instruction, more easily accessible than what can be gathered from modern characters, in whom less clearly defined temperaments and more complex conditions of life have made it harder to distinguish the characteristic features of the mind. To mention only one or two--

St. Francis of Sales and Blessed Thomas More were great assentors, so were Pico de Mirandola and the great Popes of the Renaissance, an example of a great Nonconformist is Savonarola.

The old division of temperaments into phlegmatic or lymphatic, sanguine, choleric, and nervous or melancholy, is a fairly good foundation for preliminary observation, especially as each of the four subdivides itself easily into two types--the hard and soft--reforms itself easily into some cross-divisions, and refuses to be blended into others. Thus a very fine type of character is seen when the characteristics of the sanguine and choleric are blended the qualities of one correcting the faults of the other, and a very poor one if a yielding lymphatic temperament has also a strain of melancholy to increase its tendency towards inaction. It is often easy to discern in a group of children the leading characteristics of these temperaments, the phlegmatic or lymphatic, hard or soft, not easily stirred, one stubborn and the other yielding, both somewhat immobile, generally straightforward and reliable, law abiding, accessible to reason, not exposed to great dangers nor likely to reach unusual heights. Next the sanguine, hard or soft, as hope or enjoyment have the upper hand in them; this is the richest group in attractive power. If hope is the stronger factor there is a fund of energy which, allied with the power of charm and persuasion, with trustfulness in good, and optimistic outlook on the world, wins its way and succeeds in its undertakings, making its appeal to the will rather than to the mind. On the softer side of this type are found the disappointing people who ought to do

well, and always fail, for whom the *joie de vivre*
carries everything before it, who are always good
natured, always obliging, always sweet-tempered,
who cannot say no, especially to themselves, whose
energy is exhausted in a very short burst of effort,
though ever ready to direct itself into some new
channel for as brief a trial. The characters which
remain "characters of great promise" to the end of
their days, great promise doomed to be always
unfulfilled. Of all characters, these are perhaps the
most disappointing; they have so much in their
favour, and the one thing wanting, steadiness of
purpose, renders useless their most beautiful gifts.
These two groups seem to be the most common
among the Teutons and Celts of Northern Europe
with fair colouring and tall build; perhaps the other
two types are correspondingly more numerous
among the Latin races. They are choleric,
ambitious, or self-isolated, as the cast of their mind
is eager or scornful and generally capable of
dissimulation; the world is not large enough for
their Bonapartes. But if bitterness and sadness
predominate, they are carried on an ebbing tide
towards pessimism and contemptuous weariness of
life; their soft type, in so far as they have one, has
the softness of powder, dry and crushed, rather than
that of a living organism. In children, this type,
fortunately rare, has not the charm or joy of
childhood, but shows a restless straining after some
self-centred excellence, and a coldness of affection
which indicates the isolation towards which it is
carried in later life. Lastly, there is the unquiet
group of nervous or melancholic temperaments,
their melancholy not weighed down by listless
sadness as the inactive lymphatics, but more

actively dissatisfied with things as they are--
untiringly but unhopefully at work--hard on
themselves, anxious-minded, assured that in spite of
their efforts all will turn out for the worst, often
scrupulous, capable of long-sustained efforts, often
of heroic devotedness and superhuman endurance,
for which their reward is not in this world, as the art
of pleasing is singularly deficient in them. Here are
found the people who are "so good, but so trying,"
ever in a fume and fuss, who, for sheer goodness,
rouse in others the spirit of contradiction. These
characters are at their best in adversity, trouble
stimulates them to their best efforts, whereas in easy
circumstances and surrounded with affection they
are apt to drop into querulous and exacting habits. If
they are endowed with more than ordinary energy it
is in the direction of diplomacy, and not always
frank. On the whole this is the character whose
features are least clearly defined, over which a
certain mystery hangs, and strange experiences are
not unfrequent It is difficult to deal with its elusive
showings and vanishings, and this melting away
and reappearing seems in some to become a habit
and even a matter of choice, with a determination
not to be known.

Taking these groups as a rough classification for
observation of character, it is possible to get a fair
idea of the raw material of a class, though it may be
thankfully added that in the Church no material is
really raw, with the grace of Baptism in the soul and
later on the Sacrament of Penance, to clear its
obscurities and explain it to itself and by degrees to
transform its tendencies and with grace and
guidance to give it a steady impulse towards the

better things. Confirmation and First Communion sometimes sensibly and even suddenly transfigure a character; but even apart from such choice instances the gradual work of the Sacraments brings Catholic children under a discipline in which the habit of self-examination, the constant necessity for effort, the truthful avowal of being in the wrong, the acceptance of penance as a due, the necessary submissions and self-renunciations of obedience to the Church, give a training of their own. So a practicing Catholic child is educated unconsciously by a thousand influences, each of which, supernatural in itself, tells beyond the supernatural sphere and raises the natural qualities, by self-knowledge, by truth, by the safeguard of religion against hardness and isolation and the blindness of pride, even if the minimum of educational facilities have been at work to take advantage of these openings for good. A Catholic child is a child, and keeps a childlike spirit for life, unless the early training is completely shipwrecked, and even then there are memories which are means of recovery, and the way home to the Father's house is known. It may be hoped that very many never leave it, and never lose the sense of being one of the great family, "of the household of faith." They enjoy the freedom of the house, the rights of children, the ministries of all the graces which belong to the household, the power of being at home in every place because the Church is there with its priesthood and its Sacraments, responsible for its children, and able to supply the wants of their souls. It is scarcely possible to find among Catholic children the inaccessible little bits of flint who are not *brought* up, but bring up their own souls outside the Church--proud in their isolation, most proud of never yielding inward obedience or owning themselves in the wrong, and of being sufficient for themselves. When the grace of Q-od reaches them and they are admitted into the Church, one of the most overwhelming experiences is that of becoming one of a family, for whom there is some one responsible, the Father of the family whose authority and love pass through their appointed channels, down to the least child.

There is no such thing as an orphan child within the Church, there are possibilities of training and development which belong to those who have to educate the young which must appeal particularly to Catholic teachers, for they know more than others the priceless value of the children with whom they have to do. Children, souls, freighted for their voyage through life, vessels so frail and bound for such a port are worthy of the devoted care of those who have necessarily a lifelong influence over them, and the means of using that influence for their lifelong good ought to be a matter of most earnest study. Knowledge must come before action, and first-hand knowledge, acquired by observation, is worth more than theoretic acquirements; the first may supply for the second, but not the second for the first. There are two types of educators of early childhood which no theory could produce, and indeed no theory could tell how they are produced, but they stand unrivalled--one is the English nurse and the other the Irish. The English nurse is a being apart, with a profound sense of fitness in all things, herself the slave of duty; and having certain ideals transmitted, who can tell how, by an unwritten traditional code, as to what *ought to be*, and a gift of authority by which she secures that these things *shall be*, reverence for God, reverence in prayer, reverence for parents, consideration of brothers for sisters, unselfishness, manners, etc., her views on all these things are like the laws of the Medes and Persians "which do not alter "--and they are also holy and wholesome. The Irish nurse rules by the heart, and by sympathy, by a power of self-devotion that can only be found where the love of God is the deepest love of the heart; she has no views, but--she knows. She does not need to observe--she sees' she has instincts, she never lays down a law, but she wins by tact and affection, lifting up the mind to God and subduing the will to obedience, while appearing to do nothing but love and wait. The stamp that she leaves on the earliest years of training is never entirely effaced; it remains as some instinct of faith, a habit of resignation to the will of God, and habitual recourse to prayer. Both these types of educators rule by their gift from God, and it is hard to believe that the most finished training in the art of nursery management can produce anything like them, for they govern by those things that lectures and handbooks cannot teach--faith, love, and common sense.

Those who take up the training of the next stage have usually to learn by their own experience, and study what is given to very few as a natural endowment--the art of so managing the wills of children that without provoking resistance, yet without yielding to every fancy, they may be led by degrees to self-control and to become a law to themselves. It must be recognized from the beginning that the work is slow; if it is forced on too fast either a breaking point comes and the child, too much teased into perfection, turns in reaction and becomes self-willed and rebellious; or if, unhappily, the forcing process succeeds, a little paragon is produced like Wordsworth's "model child":--

"Full early trained to worship seemliness, This model of a child is never known To mix in quarrels; that were far beneath Its dignity; with gifts he bubbles o'er As generous as a fountain; selfishness May not come near him, nor the little throng Of flitting pleasures tempt him from his path; The wandering beggars propagate his name. Dumb creatures find him tender as a nun, And natural or supernatural fear, Unless it leap upon him in a dream, Touches him not. To enhance the wonder, see How arch his notices, how nice his sense Of the ridiculous; not blind is he To the broad follies of the licensed world, Yet innocent himself withal, though shrewd, And can read lectures upon innocence; A miracle of scientific lore, Ships he can guide across the pathless sea, And tell you all their cunning; he can read The inside of the earth, and spell the stars; He knows the policies of foreign lands; Can string you names of districts, cities, towns, The whole world over, tight as beads of dew Upon a gossamer thread; he sifts, he weighs; All things are put to question; he must live Knowing that he grows wiser every day Or else not live at all, and seeing too Each little drop of wisdom as it falls Into the dimpling cistern of his heart: For this unnatural growth the trainer blame, Pity the tree,"-- "The Prelude," Bk. V, lines 298-329.

On the other hand if those who have to bring up children, fear too much to cross their inclinations, and so seek always the line of least resistance, teaching lessons in play, and smoothing over every rough peace of the road, the result is a weak, slack will, a mind without power of concentration, and in later life very little resourcefulness in emergency or power of bearing up under difficulties or privations. We are at present more inclined to produce these soft characters than to develop paragons. But such movements go in waves and the wave-lengths are growing shorter; we seem now to be reaching the end of a period when, as it has been expressed, "the teacher learns the lessons and says them to the child." We are beginning to outgrow too fervid belief in methods, and pattern lessons, and coming back to value more highly the habit of effort, individual work, and even the saving discipline of drudgery. *We* are beginning, that is those who really care for children, and for character, and for life; it takes the State and its departments a long time to come up with the experience of those who actually know living children--a generation is not too much to allow for its coming to this knowledge, as we may see at present, when the drawbacks of the system of 1870 are becoming apparent at last in the eyes of the official world, having been evident for years to those whose sympathies were with the children and not with codes. America, open-minded America, is aware of all this, and is making generous educational experiments with the buoyant idealism of a young nation, an idealism that is sometimes outstripping its practical sense, quite able to face its disappointments if they come, as undoubtedly they will, and to begin again. In one point it is far ahead of us--in the understanding that a large measure of freedom is necessary for teachers. Whereas we are, let us hope, at the most acute stage of State interference in details.

But in spite of the systems the children live, and come up year after year, to give us fresh opportunities; and in spite of the systems something can be done with them if we take the advice of Archbishop Ullathorne--"trust in God and begin as you can."

Let us begin by learning to know them, and the knowledge of their characters is more easily gained if some cardinal points are marked, by which the unknown country may be mapped out. The selection of these cardinal points depends in part on the mind of the observer, which has more or less insight into the various manifestations of possibility and quality which may occur. It is well to observe without seeming to do so, for as shy wild creatures fly off before a too observant eye, but may be studied by a naturalist who does not appear to look at them, so the real child takes to flight if it is too narrowly watched, and leaves a self conscious little person to take its place, making off with its true self into the backwoods of some dreamland, and growing more and more reticent about its real thoughts as it gets accustomed to talk to an appreciative audience. With weighing and measuring, inspecting and reporting, exercising and rapid forcing, and comparing, applauding and tabulating results, it is difficult to see how children can escape self-consciousness and artificiality, and the enthusiasts for "child study" are in danger of making the specimen of the real child more and more rare and difficult to find, as destructive sportsmen in a new country exterminate the choice species of wild animals.

Too many questions put children on their guard or make them unreal; they cannot give an account of what they think and what they mean and how far they have understood, and the greater the anxiety shown to get at their real mind the less are they either able or willing to make it known; so it is the quieter and less active observers who see the most, and those who observe most are best aware how little can be known.

Yet there are some things which may serve as points of the compass, especially in the transitional years when the features both of face and character begin to accentuate themselves. One of these is the level of friendships. There are some who look by instinct for the friendship of those above them, and others habitually seek a lower level, where there is no call to self-restraint. Boys who hang about the stables, girls who like the conversation of servants; boys and girls who make friends in sets at school, among the less desirable, generally do so from a love of ease and dislike of that restraint and effort which every higher friendship calls for; they can be *somebody* at a very cheap cost where the standard of talk is not exacting, whereas to be with those who are striving for the best in any station makes demands which call for exertion, and the taste for this higher level, the willingness to respond to its claims, give good promise that those who have it will in their turn draw others to the things that are best.

The attitude of a child towards books is also
indicative of the whole background of a mind; the
very way in which a book is handled is often a sign
in itself of whether a child is a citizen born, or an
alien, in the world for which books stand. Taste in
reading, both as to quality and quantity, is so
obviously a guiding line that it need scarcely be
mentioned.

Play is another line in which character shows itself,
and reveals another background against which the
scenes of life in the future will stand out, and in
school life the keenest and best spirits will generally
divide into these two groups, the readers and the
players, with a few, rarely gifted, who seem to excel
in both. From the readers will come those who are
to influence the minds of others here, if they do not
let themselves be carried out too far to keep in
touch with real life. From the players will come
those whose gift is readiness and decision in action,
if they on their side do not remain mere players
when life calls for something more.

There are other groups, the born artists with their
responsive minds, the "home children" for whom
everything centres in their own home-world, and
who have in them the making of another one in the
future; the critics, standing aloof, a little peevish
and very self-conscious, hardly capable of deep
friendship and fastidiously dissatisfied with people
and things in general; the cheerful and helpful souls
who have no interests of their own but can devote
themselves to help anyone; the opposite class whose

life is in their own moods and feelings. Many others
might be added, each observer's experience can
supply them, and will probably close the list with
the same little group, the very few, that stand a little
apart, but not aloof, children of privilege, with
heaven in their eyes and a little air of mystery about
them, meditative and quiet, friends of God, friends
of all, loved and loving, and asking very little from
the outer world, because they have more than
enough within. They are classed as the dreamers,
but they are really the seers. They do not ask much
and they do not need much beyond a reverent
guardianship, and to be let alone and allowed to
grow; they will find their way for they are "taught
of God."

It is impossible to do more than to throw out
suggestions which any child-naturalist might
multiply or improve upon. The next consideration
for all concerned is what to do with the acquired
knowledge, and how to "bring up" in the later
stages of childhood and early youth.

What do we want to bring up? Not good
nonentities, who are merely good because they are
not bad. There are too many of them already, no
trouble to anyone, only disappointing, so good that
they ought to be so much better, if only they *would*.
But who can make them will to be something more,
to become, as Montalembert said, "a *fact*, instead of
remaining but a shadow, an echo, or a ruin?" Those
who have to educate them to something higher must
themselves have an idea of what they want; they
must believe in the possibility of every mind and
character to be lifted up to something better than it

has already attained; they must themselves be striving for some higher excellence, and must believe and care deeply for the things they teach. For no one can be educated by maxim and precept; it is the life lived, and the things loved and the ideals believed in, by which we tell, one upon another. If we care for energy we call it out; if we believe in possibilities of development we almost seem to create them. If we want integrity of character, steadiness, reliability, courage, thoroughness, all the harder qualities that serve as a backbone, we, at least, make others want them also, and strive for them by the power of example that is not set as deliberate good example, for that is as tame as a precept, but the example of the life that is lived, and the truths that are honestly believed in.

The gentler qualities which are to adorn the harder virtues may be more explicitly taught. It is always more easy to tone down than to brace up; there must fist be something to moderate, before moderation can be a virtue; there must be strength before gentleness can be taught, as there must be some hardness in material things to make them capable of polish. And these are qualities which are specially needed in our unsteady times, when rapid emancipation of unknown forces makes each one more personally responsible than in the past. It is an impatient age: we must learn patience; it is an age of sudden social changes: we have to make ready for adversity; it is an age of lawlessness: each one must stand upon his own guard and be his own defence; it is a selfish age, and never was unselfishness more urgently needed; love of home and love of country seem to be cooling, one as rapidly as the other: never was it more necessary to learn the spirit of self-sacrifice both for family life and the love and honour due to one's country which is also "piety" in its true sense.

All these things come with our Catholic faith and practice if it is rightly understood. Catholic family life, Catholic citizenship, Catholic patriotism are the truest, the only really true, because the only types of these virtues that are founded on truth. But they do not come of themselves. Many will let themselves be carried to heaven, as they hope, in the long-suffering arms of the Church without either defending or adorning her by their virtues, and we shall but add to their number if we do not kindle in the minds of children the ambition to do something more, to devote themselves to the great Cause, by self-sacrifice to be in some sort initiated into its spirit, and identified with it, and thus to make it worth while for others as well as for themselves that they have lived their life on earth. There is a price to be paid for this, and they must face it; a good life cannot be a soft life, and a great deal, even of innocent pleasure, has to be given up, voluntarily, to make life worth living, if it were only as a training in *doing without.*

Independence is a primary need for character, and independence can only be learnt by doing without pleasant things, even unnecessarily. Simplicity of life is an essential for greatness of life, and the very meaning of the simple life is the laying aside of many things which tend to grow by habit into necessities. The habit of work is another necessity in any life worth living, and this is only learnt by refraining again and again from what is pleasant for the sake of what is precious. Patience and thoroughness are requirements whose worth and value never come home to the average mind until they are seen in startling excellence, and it is apparent what a price must have been paid to acquire their adamant perfection, a lesson which might be the study of a lifetime. The value of time is another necessary lesson of the better life, a hard lesson, but one that makes an incalculable difference between the expert and the untried. We are apt to be always in a hurry now, for obvious reasons which hasten the movement of life, but not many really know how to use time to the full. Our tendency is to alternate periods of extreme activity with intervals of complete prostration for recovery. Perhaps our grandparents knew better in a slower age the use of time. The old Marquise de Gramont, aged 93, after receiving Extreme Unction, asked for her knitting, for the poor. "Mais Madame la Marquise a ete administree, elle va mourir!" said the maid, who thought the occupation of dying sufficient for a lady of her age. "Ma chere, ce n'est pas une raison pour perdre son temps," answered the indomitable Marquise. It is told of her also that when one of her children asked for some water in summer, between meals, she replied: "Mon enfant, vous ne serez jamais qu'un etre manque, une pygmee, si vous prenez ces habitudes-la, pensez, mon petit coeur, au fiel de Notre Seigneur Jesus Christ, et vous aurez le courage d'attendre le diner." She had learned for herself the strength of *going without*.

One more lesson must be mentioned, the hardest of

all to be learnt--perfect sincerity. It is so hard not to pose, for all but the very truest and simplest natures--to pose as independent, being eaten up with human respect; to pose as indifferent though aching with the wish to be understood; to pose as flippant while longing to be in earnest; to hide an attraction to higher things under a little air of something like irreverence. It is strange that this kind of pose is considered as less insincere than the opposite class, which is rather out of fashion for this very reason, yet to be untrue to one's better self is surely an unworthier insincerity than to be ashamed of the worst. Perhaps the best evidence of this is the costliness of the effort to overcome it, and the more observation and reflection we spend on this point the more shall we be convinced that it is very hard to learn to be quite true, and that it entails more personal self-sacrifice than almost any other virtue.

In conclusion, the means for training character may be grouped under the following headings:--

1. Contact with those who have themselves attained to higher levels, either parent, or teacher, or friend. Perhaps at present the influence of a friend is greater than that of any power officially set over us, so jealous are we of control. So much the better chance for those who have the gift even in mature age of winning the friendship of children, and those who have just outgrown childhood. In these friendships the great power of influence is hopefulness, to believe in possibilities of good, and to expect the best.

2. Vigilance, not the nervous vigilance, unquiet and

anxious, which rouses to mischief the sporting instinct of children and stings the rebellious to revolt, but the vigilance which, open and confident itself, gives confidence, nurtures fearlessness, and brings a steady pressure to be at one's best. Vigilance over children is no insult to their honour, it is rather the right of their royalty, for they are of the blood royal of Christianity, and deserve the guard of honour which for the sake of their royalty does not lose sight of them.

3. Criticism and correction. To be used with infinite care, but never to be neglected without grave injustice. It is not an easy thing to reprove in the right time, in the right tone, without exasperation, without impatience, without leaving a sting behind; to dare to give pain for the sake of greater good; to love the truth and have courage to tell it; to change reproof as time goes on to the frank criticism of friendship that is ambitious for its friend. To accept criticism is one of the greatest lessons to be learnt in life. To give it well is an art which requires more study and more self-denial than either the habit of being easily satisfied and requiring little, or the querulous habit of "scolding" which is admirably described by Bishop Hedley as "the resonance of the empty intelligence and of the hollow heart of the man who has nothing to give, nothing to propose, nothing to impart."

4. Discipline and obedience. If these are to be means of training they must be living and not dead powers, and they must lead up to gradual self-government, not to sudden emancipation. Obedience must be first of all to persons, prompt

and unquestioning, then to laws, a "reasonable service," then to the wider law which each one must enforce from within--the law of love which is the law of liberty of the kingdom of God.

These are the means which in her own way, and through various channels of authority, the Church makes use of, and the Church is the great Mother who educates us all. She takes us into her confidence, as we make ourselves worthy of it, and shows us out of her treasures things new and old. She sets the better things always before us, prays for us, prays with us, teaches us to pray, and so "lifts up our minds to heavenly desires." She watches over us with un anxious, but untiring vigilance, setting her Bishops and pastors to keep watch over the flock, collectively and individually, "with that most perfect care" that St. Francis of Sales describes as "that which approaches the nearest to the care God has of us, which is a care full of tranquillity and quietness, and which, in its highest activity, has still no emotion, and being only one, yet condescends to make itself all to all things."

Criticism and correction, discipline and obedience-- these things are administered by the Church our Mother, gently but without weakness, so careful is she in her warnings, so slow in her punishments, so unswervingly true to what is of principle, and asking so persuasively not for the sullen obedience of slaves, but for the free and loving submission of sons and daughters.

CHAPTER III.

CHARACTER II.

"The Parts and Signes of Goodnesse are many. If a
Man be Gracious and Curteous to Strangers, it
shewes he is a Citizen of the World, And that his
Heart is no Island cut off from other Lands, but a
Continent that joynes to them. If he be
Compassionate towards the Afflictions of others, it
shewes that his Heart is like the noble Tree, that is
wounded to selfe when it gives Balme. If he easily
Pardons and Remits Offences, it shewes that his
minde is planted above Injuries, So that he cannot
be shot. If he be Thankfull for small Benefits, it
shewes that he weighes Men's Mindes, and not their
Trash. But above all, if he have St. Paul's
Perfection, that he would wish to be an Anathema
from Christ, for the Salvation of his Brethren, it
shewes much of a Divine Nature, and a kinde of
Conformity with Christ himselfe."--BACON, "Of
Goodnesse."

No one who has the good of children at heart, and
the training of their characters, can leave the subject
without some grave thoughts on the formation of
their own character, which is first in order of
importance, and in order of time must go before,
and accompany their work to the very end.

"What is developed to perfection can make other
things like unto itself." So saints develop sanctity in
others, and truth and confidence beget truth and
confidence, and the spirit of enterprise calls out the
spirit of enterprise, and constancy trains to

endurance and perseverance, and wise kindness
makes others kind, and courage makes them
courageous, and in its degree each good quality
tends to reproduce itself in others. Children are very
delicately sensitive to these influences, they respond
unconsciously to what is expected of them, and
instinctively they imitate the models set before
them. They catch a tone, a gesture, a trick of
manner with a quickness that is startling. The
influence of mind and thought on mind and thought
cannot be so quickly recognized, but tells with as
much certainty, and enters more deeply into the
character for life. The consideration of this is a
great incentive to the acquirement of self-
knowledge and self-discipline by those who have to
do with children. The old codes of conventionality
in education, which stood for a certain system in
their time, are disappearing, and the worth of the
individual becomes of greater importance. This is
true of those who educate and of those whom they
bring up. As the methods of modern warfare call for
more individual resourcefulness, so do the methods
of the spiritual warfare, now that we are not
supported by big battalions, but each one is thrown
back on conscience and personal responsibility.
Girls as well as boys have to be trained to take care
of themselves and be responsible for themselves,
and if they are not so trained, no one can now be
responsible for them or protect them in spite of
themselves. Therefore, the first duty of those who
are bringing up Catholic girls is to be themselves
such as Catholic girls must be later on. This
example is a discourse "in the vulgar tongue" which
cannot be misunderstood, and example is not
resented unless it seems self-conscious and

presented of set purpose. The one thing necessary is to be that which we ought to be, and that is to say, in other words, that the fundamental virtue in teaching children is a great and resolute sincerity. Sincerity is a difficult virtue to practise and is too easily taken for granted. It has more enemies than appear at first sight. Inertness of mind, the desire to do things cheaply, dislike of mental effort, the tendency to be satisfied with appearances, the wish to shine, impatience for results, all foster intellectual insincerity; just as, in conduct, the wish to please, the spirit of accommodation and expediency, the fear of blame, the instinct of concealment, which is inborn in many girls, destroy frankness of character and make people untrue who would not willingly be untruthful. Yet even truthfulness is not such a matter of course as many would be willing to assume. To be inaccurate through thoughtless laziness in the use of words is extremely common, to exaggerate according to the mood of the moment, to say more than one means and cover one's retreat with "I didn't mean it," to pull facts into shape to suit particular ends, are demoralizing forms of untruthfulness, common, but often unrecognized. If a teacher could only excel in one high quality for training girls, probably the best in which she could excel would be a great sincerity, which would train them in frankness, and in the knowledge that to be entirely frank means to lay down a great price for that costly attainment, a perfectly honourable and fearless life. [1--"A woman, if it be once known that she is deficient in truth, has no resource. Have, by a misuse of language, injured or lost her only means of persuasion, nothing can preserve her from falling

into contempt of nonentity. When she is no longer
to be believed no on will take the trouble to listen to
her...no one can depend on her, no on rests any
hope on her, the words of which she makes use
have no meaning." --Madame Necker de Saussure,
"Progressive Education."]

It sometimes happens that the realization of this
truth comes comparatively late in life to those who
ought to have recognized it years before. Thinking
along the surface of things, and in particular
repeating catchwords and platitudes and trite
maxims on the subject of sincerity, is apt to make us
believe that we possess the quality we talk about,
and as it is impossible to have anything to do with
the education of children without treating of
sincerity and truthfulness, it is comparatively easy
to slip into the happy assumption that one is
truthful, because one would not deliberately be
otherwise. But it takes far more than this to acquire
real sincerity of life in the complexity and
artificiality of the conditions in which we live.

"And we have been on many thousand lines, And
we have shown, on each, spirit and power; But
hardly have we, for one little hour, Been on our
own line, have we been ourselves.

"Our hidden self, and what we say and do Is
eloquent, is well--but 'tis not true!" MATTHEW
ARNOLD, "The Buried Life."

Sincerity requires the recognition that to be
honestly oneself is more impressive for good than to
be a very superior person by imitation. It requires

the renunciation of some claims to consideration and esteem, and the acceptance of limitations (a different thing from acquiescence in them, for it means the acceptance of a lifelong effort to be what we aspire to be, with a knowledge that we shall never fully attain it). It requires that we should bear the confusion of defeat without desisting from the struggle, that we should accept the progressive illumination of what is still unaccomplished, and keep the habitual lowliness of a beginner with the unconquerable hopefulness which comes of a fixed resolution to win what is worth winning. Let those who have tried say whether this is easy.

But in guiding children along this difficult way it is not wise to call direct attention to it, lest their inexperience and sensitiveness should turn to scrupulosity and their spontaneity be paralysed. It is both more acceptable and healthier to present it as a feat of courage, a habit of fearlessness to be acquired, of hardihood and strength of character. The more subtle forms of self-knowledge belong to a later period in life.

Another quality to be desired in those who have to do with children is what may--for want of a better word--be called vitality, not the fatiguing artificial animation which is sometimes assumed professionally by teachers, but the keenness which shows forth a settled conviction that life is worth living. The expression of this is not self asserting or controversial, for it is not like a garment put on, but a living grace of soul, coming from within, born of straight thinking and resolution, and so strongly confirmed by faith and hope that nothing can

discourage it or make it let go. It is a bulwark
against the faults which sink below the normal line
of life, dullness, depression, timidity,
procrastination, sloth and sadness, moodiness,
unsociability--all these it tends to dispel, by its quiet
and confident gift of encouragement. And though so
contrary to the spirit of childhood, these faults are
found in children--often in delicate children who
have lost confidence in themselves from being
habitually outdone by stronger brothers and sisters,
or in slow minds which seem "stupid" to others and
to themselves, or in natures too sensitive to risk
themselves in the melee. To these, one who brings
the gift of encouragement comes as a deliverer and
often changes the course of their life, leading them
to believe in themselves and their own good
endowments, making them taste success which
rouses them to better efforts, giving them the strong
comfort of knowing that something is expected of
them, and that if they will only try, in one way if not
in another, they need not be behind the best. At
some stage in life, and especially in the years of
rapid growth, we all need encouragement, and often
characters that seem to require only repression are
merely singing out of tune from the effort to hold
out against blank discouragement at their failures to
"be good," or to divert their mind forcibly from
their fits of depression. To be scolded accentuates
their trouble and tends to harden them; to grow a
shell of hardness seems for the moment their only
defence; but if some one will meet their efforts half-
way, believing in them with a tranquil conviction
that they will live through these difficulties and *find
themselves* in due time, they can be saved from
much unhappiness of their own making, though not

of their own fault, and their growth will not be arrested behind an unnatural shell of defence.

The strong vitality and gift of encouragement which can give this help are also of value in saving from the morbid and exaggerated friendships which sometimes spoil the best years of a girl's education. If the character of those who teach them has force enough not only to inspire admiration but to call out effort, it may rouse the mind and will to a higher plane and make the things of which it disapproves seem worthless. There are moments when the leading mind must have strength enough for two, but this must not last. Its glory is to raise the mind of the learner to equality with itself, not to keep it in leading strings, but to make it grow so that, as the master has often been outstripped by the scholar, the efforts of the younger may even stimulate the achievements of the elder, and thus a noble friendship be formed in the pursuit of what is best.

Educators of youth are exposed to certain professional dangers, which lie very close to professional excellences of character. There is the danger of remaining young for the sake of children, so that something of mature development will be lacking. If there is not a stimulus from outside, and it is not supplied for by an inward determination to grow, the mental development may be arrested and contented-ness at a low level be mistaken for the limit of capacity. A great many people are mentally lazy, and only too ready to believe that they can do no more.

Many teachers are yoked to an examination

programme sufficiently loaded to call for a great deal of pressure along a low level, and they may easily mistake this harassing activity for real mental work, and either be indeed hindered, or consider themselves absolved from anything more. The penalty of it is a gradual decline of the unused powers, growing difficulty of sustained attention, dislike for what requires effort of mind, loss of wider interests, restlessness and superficiality in reading, and other indications of diminution of power in the years when it ought to be on the increase. Is this the fault of those who so decline in power? It would be hard to say that it is so universally, for some no doubt are pressed through necessity to the very limits of their time and of their endurance. Yet experience goes to prove that if a mental awakening really takes place the most unfavourable circumstances will not hinder a rapid development of power. Abundance of books and leisure and fostering conditions are helps but not essentials for mental growth. If few books can be had, but these are of the best, they will do more for the mind by continued reading than abundance for those who have not yet learned to use it. If there is little leisure the value of the hardly-spared moments is enhanced; we may convince ourselves of this in the lives of those who have reached eminence in learning, through circumstances apparently hopeless. If the conditions of life are unfavourable, it is generally possible to find one like-minded friend who will double our power by quickening enthusiasm or by setting the pace at which we must travel, and leading the way. There may be side by side in the same calling in life persons doing similar work in like circumstances, with like resources, of

whom one is contentedly stagnating, feeling
satisfied all the time that duty is done and nothing
neglected--and this may be true up to a certain
point--while the other is haunted by a blessed
dissatisfaction, urged from within to seek always
something better, and compelling circumstances to
minister to the growth of the mind. One who would
meet these two again after the interval of a few
months would be astonished at the distance which
has been left between them by the stagnation of one
and the advance of the other.

Another danger is that of becoming dogmatic and
dictatorial from the habit of dealing with less
mature intelligences, from the absence of
contradiction and friction among equals, and the
want of that most perfect discipline of the mind--
intercourse with intellectual superiors. Of course it
is a mark of ignorance to become oracular and self-
assured, but it needs watchfulness to guard against
the tendency if one is always obliged to take the
lead. Teaching likewise exposes to faults perhaps
less in themselves but far reaching in their effect
upon children; a little observation will show how
the smallest peculiarities tell upon them, either by
affecting their dispositions or being caught by them
and reproduced. To take one example among many,
the pitch and intonation of the voice often impress
more than the words. A nurse with a querulous tone
has a restless nursery; she makes the high-spirited
contradictory and the delicate fretful. In teaching, a
high-pitched voice is exciting and wearing to
children; certain cadences that end on a high note
rouse opposition, a monotonous intonation wearies,
deeper and more ample tones are quieting and

reassuring, but if their solemnity becomes exaggerated they provoke a reaction. Most people have a certain cadence which constantly recurs in their speaking and is characteristic of them, and the satisfaction of listening to them depends largely upon this characteristic cadence. It is also a help in the understanding of their characters. Much trouble of mind is saved by recognizing that a certain cadence which sounds indignant is only intended to be convincing, and that another which sounds defiant is only giving to itself the signal for retreat. Again, for the teacher's own sake, it is good to observe that there are tones which dispose towards obedience, and others which provoke remonstrance and, as Mme. Necker de Saussure remarks: "It is of great consequence to prevent remonstrances and not allow girls to form a habit of contradicting and cavilling, or to prolong useless opposition which annoys others and disturbs their own peace of mind."

There are "teacher's manners" in many varieties, often spoiling admirable gifts and qualities, for the professional touch in this is not a grace but puts both children and "grown-ups" on the defensive. There is the head mistress's manner which is a signal to proceed with caution, the modern "form mistress's" or class mistress's manner, with an off-hand tone destined to reassure by showing that there is nothing to be afraid of, the science mistress's manner with a studied quietness and determination that the knife-edge of the balance shall be the standard of truthfulness, the professionally encouraging manner, the "stimulating" manner, the manner of those whose ambition is to be "an earnest

teacher," the strained tone of one whose ideal is to
to be overworked, the kindergarten manner,
scientifically "awakening," giving the call of the
decoy-duck, confidentially inviting co operation
and revealing secrets--these are types, but there are
many others.

Such mannerisms would seem to be developed by
reliance on books of method, by professional
training imparted to those who have not enough
originality to break through the mould, and instead
of following out principles as lines for personal
experiment and discovery, deaden them into rules
and abide by them. The teacher's manner is much
more noticeable among those who have been
trained than among the now vanishing class of those
who have had to stand or fall by their own merits,
and find out their own methods. The advantage is
not always with the trained teacher even now, and
the question of manner is not one of minor
importance. The true instinct of children and the
sensitiveness of youth detect very quickly and
resent a professional tone; a child looks for freedom
and simplicity, and feels cramped if it meets with
something even a little artificial. Children like to
find *real people*, not anxiously careful to improve
them, but able to take life with a certain spontaneity
as they like to take it themselves. They are
frightened by those who take themselves too
seriously, who are too acute, too convincing or too
brilliant; they do not like people who appear to be
always on the alert, nor those of extreme
temperatures, very ardent or very frigid. The people
whom they like and trust are usually quiet, simple
people, who have not startling ways, and do not

manifest those strenuous ideals which destroy all sense of leisure in life.

Not only little children but those who are growing up resent these mannerisms and professional ways. They, too, ask for a certain spontaneity and like to find a *real person* whom they can understand. Abstract principles do not appeal to them, but they can understand and appreciate character, not in one type and pattern alone, for every character that has life and truth commands their respect and is acceptable in one way if not in another. It is not the bright colours of character alone which attract them, they often keep a lifelong remembrance of those whose qualities are anything but showy. They look for fairness in those who govern them, but if they find this they can accept a good measure of severity. They respect unflinching uprightness and are quick to detect the least deviation from it. They prefer to be taken seriously on their own ground; things in general are so incomprehensible that it only makes matters worse to be approached with playful methods and facetious invitations into the unknown, for who can tell what educational ambush for their improvement may be concealed behind these demonstrations. They give their confidence more readily to grave and quiet people who do not show too rapturous delight in their performances, or surprise at their opinions, or--especially--distress at their ignorance. They admire with lasting admiration those who are hard on themselves and take their troubles without comment or complaint. They admire courage, and they can appreciate patience if it does not seem to be conscious of itself. But they do not look up to a character in which mildness so predominates that it cannot be roused to indignation and even anger in a good cause. A power of being roused is felt as a force in reserve, and the knowledge that it is there is often enough to maintain peace and order without any need for interference or remonstrance. They are offended by a patience which looks like weariness, determined if it were at the last gasp to "improve the occasion" and say something of educational profit. To "improve the occasion" really destroys the opportunity; it is like a too expansive invitation to birds to come and feed, which drives them off in a nutter. Birds come most willingly when crumbs are thrown as it were by accident while the benefactor looks another way; and young minds pick up gratefully a suggestion which seems to fall by the way, a mere hint that things are understood and cared about, that there is safety beyond the thin ice if one trusts and believes, that "all shall be well" if people will be true to their best thoughts. They can understand these assurances and accept them when something more explicit would drive them back to bar the door against intruders. All these are truisms to those who have observed children. The misfortune is that in spite of the prominence given to training of teachers, of the new name of "Child Study" and its manuals, there are many who teach children without reaching their real selves. If the children could combine the result of their observations and bring out a manual of "Teacher Study" we should have strange revelations as to how it looks from the other side. We should be astonished at the shrewdness of the small juries that deliberate, and the insight of the judges that pronounce sentence upon us, and we should be convinced that to obtain a favourable verdict we needed very little subtlety, and not too much theory, but as much as possible of the very things we look for as the result and crown of our work. We labour to produce character, we must have it. We look for courage and uprightness, we must bring them with us. We want honest work, we have to give proof of it ourselves. And so with the Christian qualities which we hope to build on these foundations. We care for the faith of the children, it must abound in us. We care for the innocence of their life, we must ourselves be heavenly minded, we want them to be unworldly and ready to make sacrifices for their religion, they must understand that it is more than all the world to us. We want to secure them as they grow up against the spirit of pessimism, our own imperturbable hope in God and confidence in the Church will be more convincing than our arguments. We want them to grow into the fulness of charity, we must make charity the most lovable and lovely thing in the world to them.

The Church possesses the secrets of these things; she is the great teacher of all nations and brings out of her treasury things new and old for the training of her children. A succession of teaching orders of religious, representing different patterns of education, has gone forth with her blessing to supply the needs of succeeding generations in each class of the Christian community. When children cannot be brought up in their own homes, religious seem to be designated as their natural guardians, independent as they are by their profession from the claims of personal interest and self-advancement, and therefore free to give their full sympathy and devotion to the children under their charge. They have also the independence of their corporate life, a great power behind the service of the schoolroom in which they find mutual support, an "Upper Boom" to which they can withdraw and build up again in prayer and intercourse with one another their ideals of life and duty in an atmosphere which gives a more spiritual re-renewal of energy than a holiday of entire forgetfulness.

It is striking to observe that while the so-called Catholic countries are banishing religious from their schools, there is more and more inclination among non-Catholic parents who have had experience of other systems to place their children under the care of religious. And it was strange to hear one of His Majesty's Inspectors express his conviction that "it would be ideal if all England could be taught by nuns!" Thus indirect testimony comes from friendly or hostile sources to the fact that the Church holds the secret of education, and every Catholic teacher may gain courage from the knowledge of having that which is beyond all price in the education of children, that which all the world is seeking for, and which the Church alone knows that she possesses in its fulness.

CHAPTER IV.

THE ELEMENTS OF CATHOLIC PHILOSOPHY.

"E quosto ti sia sempre piombo ai piedi, Per farti
mover lento, com' uom lasso, Ed al si ed al no, che
tu non vedi; Che quegli e tra gli stolti bene abbasso,
Che senza disfcinzion afferma o nega, Nell' un cosi
come nell' altro passo; Perch' egl' incontra che piu
volte piega L' opinion corrente in falsa parte, E poi
l' affetto lo intelletto lega. Vie piu che indarno da
riva si parte, Perche non toma tal qual ei si move,
Chi pesca per lo vero e noil ha l' arte." DANTE,
"Paradiso," Canto XIII.

The elements of Catholic philosophy may no longer
be looked upon as out of place in the education of
our girls, or as being reserved for the use of learned
women and girlish oddities. They belong to every
well-grounded Catholic education, and the need for
them will be felt more and more. They are wanted
to balance on the one hand the unthinking impulse
of living for the day, which asks no questions so
long as the "fun" holds out, and on the other to meet
the urgency of problems which press upon the
minds of the more thoughtful as they grow up.
When this teaching has been long established as
part of an educational plan it has been found to give
steadiness and unity to the whole; something to aim
at from the beginning, and in the later years of a
girl's education something which will serve as
foundation for all branches of future study, so that
each will find its place among the first principles,
not isolated from the others but as part of a whole.
The value of these elements for the practical

guidance of life is likewise very great. A hold is given in the mind to the teaching of religion and conduct which welds into one defence the best wisdom of this world and of the next. For instance, the connexion between reason and faith being once established, the fear of permanent disagreement between the two, which causes so much panic and disturbance of mind, is set at rest.

There is a certain risk at the outset of these studies that girls will take the pose of philosophical students, and talk logic and metaphysics, to the confusion of their friends and of their own feelings later on, when they come to years of discretion and realize the absurdity of these "lively sallies," as they would have been called in early Victorian times-- the name alone might serve as a warning to the incautious! They may perhaps go through an argumentative period and trample severely upon the opinions of those who are not ready to have their majors "distinguished" and their minors "conceded," and, especially, their conclusions denied. But these phases will be outlived and the hot-and-cold remembrance of them will be sufficient expiation, with the realization that they did not know much when they had taken in the "beggarly elements" which dazzled them for a moment. The more thoughtful minds will escape the painful phase altogether.

There are three special classes among girls whose difficulties of mind call for attention. There are those who frisk playfully along, taking the good things of life as they come--"the more the better"-- whom, as children, it is hard to call to account.

They are lightly impressed and only for a moment
by the things they feel, and scarcely moved at all by
the things they understand. The only side which
seems troublesome in their early life is that there is
so little hold upon it. They are unembarrassed and
quite candid about their choice; it is the enjoyable
good, life on its pleasantest side. And this
disposition is in the mind as well as in the will; they
cannot see it in any other way. Restraint galls them,
and their inclination is not to resist but to evade it.
These are kitten-like children in the beginning, and
they appear charming. But when the kitten in them
is overgrown, its playful evasiveness takes an ugly
contour and shows itself as want of principle. The
tendency to snatch at enjoyment hardens into a
grasping sense of market values, and conscience,
instead of growing inexorable, learns to be pliant to
circumstances. Debts weigh lightly, and duties
scarcely weigh at all. Concealment and untruthfulness come in very easily to save the
situation in a difficulty, and once the conduct of life
is on the down-grade it slides quickly and far, for
the sense of responsibility is lacking and these
natures own no bond of obligation. They have their
touch of piety in childhood, but it soon wears off,
and in its best days cannot stand the demands made
upon it by duty; it fails of its hold upon the soul,
like a religion without a sacrifice. In these minds
some notions of ethics leave a barbed arrow of
remorse which penetrates further than piety. They
may soothe themselves with the thought that God
will easily forgive, later on, but they cannot quite
lose consciousness of the law which does not
forgive, of the responsibility of human acts and the
inevitable punishment of wrong-doing which works

itself out, till it calls for payment of the last farthing. And by this rough way of remorse they may come back to God. Pope Leo XIII spoke of it as their best hope, an almost certain means of return. The beautiful also may make its appeal to these natures on their best side, and save them preventively from themselves, but only if the time of study is prolonged enough for the laws of order and beauty to be made comprehensible to them, so that if they admire the best, remorse may have another hold and reproach them with a lowered ideal.

In opposition to these are the minds to which, as soon as they become able to think for themselves, all life is a puzzle, and on every side, wherever they turn, they are baffled by unanswerable questions. These questions are often more insistent and more troublesome because they cannot be asked, they have not even taken shape in the mind. But they haunt and perplex it. Are they the only ones who do not know? Is it clear to every one else? This doubt makes it difficult even to hint at the perplexity. These are often naturally religious minds, and outside the guidance of the Catholic Church, in search of truth, they easily fall under the influence of different schools of thought which take them out of their depth, and lead them further and further from the reasonable certainty about first principles which they are in search of. Within the Church, of course, they can never stray so far, and the truths of faith supply their deepest needs. But if they want to know more, to know something of themselves, and to have at least some rational knowledge of the universe, then to give them a hold on the elements

of philosophical knowledge is indeed a mental if
not a spiritual work of mercy, for it enables them to
set their ideas in order by the light of a few first
principles, it shows them on what plane their
questions lie, it enables them to see how all
knowledge and new experience have connexions
with what has gone before, and belong to a whole
with a certain fitness and proportion. They learn
also thus to take themselves in hand in a reasonable
way; they gain some power of attributing effects to
their true causes, so as neither to be unduly alarmed
nor elated at the various experiences through which
they will pass.

Between these two divisions lies a large group, that
of the "average person," not specially flighty and
not particularly thoughtful. But the average person
is of very great importance. The greatest share in
the work of the world is probably done by "average"
people, not only for the obvious reason that there
are more of them, but also because they are more
accessible, more reliable, and more available for all
kinds of responsibility than those who have made
themselves useless by want of principle, or those
whose genius carries them away from the ordinary
line. They are accessible because their fellow-
creatures are not afraid of them; they are not too
fine for ordinary wear, nor too original to be able to
follow a line laid down for them, and if they take a
line of their own it is usually intelligible to others.

To these valuable "average" persons the importance
of some study of the elements of philosophy is very
great. They can hardly go through an elementary
course of mental science without wishing to learn

more, and being lifted to a higher plane. The weak
point in the average person is a tendency to sink
into the commonplace, because the consciousness
of not being brilliant induces timidity, and timidity
leads to giving up effort and accepting a fancied
impossibility of development which from being
supposed, assumed, and not disturbed, becomes in
the end real.

On the other hand the strong point of the average
person is very often common sense, that singular,
priceless gift which gives a touch of likeness among
those who possess it in all classes, high or low--in
the sovereign, the judge, the ploughman, or the
washerwoman, a likeness that is somewhat like a
common language among them and makes them
almost like a class apart. Minds endowed with
common sense are an aristocracy among the
"average," and if this quality of theirs is lifted above
the ordinary round of business and trained in the
domain of thought it becomes a sound and wide
practical judgment. It will observe a great sobriety
in its dealings with the abstract; the concrete is its
kingdom, but it will rule the better for having its
ideas systematized, and its critical power
developed. Self-diffidence tends to check this
unduly, and it has to be strengthened in reasonably
supporting its own opinion which is often
instinctively true, but fails to find utterance. It is a
help to such persons if they can learn to follow the
workings of their own mind and gain confidence in
their power to understand, and find some
intellectual interest in the drudgery which in every
order of things, high or low, is so willingly handed
over to their good management. These results may

not be showy, but it is a great thing to strengthen an "average" person, and the reward of doing so is sometimes the satisfaction of seeing that average mind rise in later years quite above the average and become a tower of steady reflection; while to itself it is a new life to gain a view of things as a whole, to find that nothing stands alone, but that the details which it grasps in so masterly a manner have their place and meaning in the scheme of the universe.

It is evident that even this elementary knowledge cannot be given in the earliest years of the education of girls, and that it is only possible to attempt it in schools and school-rooms where they can be kept on for a longer time of study. Every year that can be added to the usual course is of better value, and more appreciated, except by those who are restless to come out as soon as possible. No reference is made here to those exceptional cases in which girls are allowed to begin a course of study at a time when the majority have been obliged to finish their school life.

As the elements of philosophy are not ordinarily found in the curriculum of girls' schools or schoolroom plans, it may not be out of place to say a few words on the method of bringing the subject within their reach.

In the first place it should be kept in view from the beginning, and some preparation be made for it even in teaching the elements of subjects which are most elementary. Thus the study of any grammar may serve remotely as an introduction to logic, even English grammar which, beyond a few rudiments, is a most disinterested study, valuable for its by-products more than for its actual worth. But the practice of grammatical analysis is certainly a preparation for logic, as logic is a preparation for the various branches of philosophy. Again some preliminary exercises in definition, and any work of the like kind which gives precision in the use of language, or clear ideas of the meanings of words, is preparatory work which trains the mind in the right direction. In the same way the elements of natural science may at least set the thoughts and inquiries of children on the right track for what will later on be shown to them as the "disciplines" of cosmology and pyschology.

To make preparatory subjects serve such a purpose it is obviously required that the teachers of even young children should have been themselves trained in these studies, so far at least as to know what they are aiming at, to be able to lay foundations which will not require to be reconstructed. It is not the matter so much as the habits of mind and work that are remotely prepared in the early stages, but without some knowledge of what is coming afterwards this preparation cannot be made. In order of arrangement it is not possible for the different branches to be taught to girls according to their normal sequence; they have to be adapted to the capacity of the minds and their degree of development. Some branches cannot even be attempted during the school-room years, except so far as to prepare the mind incidentally during the study of other branches. The explanation of certain terms and fundamental notions will serve as points of departure when opportunities for development are accessible later on, as architects set "toothings" at the angles of buildings that they may be bonded into later constructions. By this means the names of the more abstruse branches are kept out of sight, and it is emphasized that the barest elements alone are within reach at present, so that the permanent impression may be--not "how much I have learned," but "how little I know and how much there is to learn." This secures at least a fitting attitude of mind in those who will never go further, and increases the thirst of those who really want more.

The most valuable parts of philosophy in the education of girls are:--

1. Those which belong to the practical side--logic, for thought; ethics, for conduct; aesthetics, for the study of the arts.

2. In speculative philosophy the "disciplines" which are most accessible and most necessary are psychology, and natural theology which is the very crown of all that they are able to learn.

General metaphysics and cosmology, and in pyschology the subordinate treatises of criteriology and idealogy are beyond their scope.

Logic, as a science, is not a suitable introduction, though some general notions on the subject are necessary as preliminary instructions. Cardinal Mercier presents these under "propaedeutics," even for his grown-up scholars, placing logic properly so called in its own rank as the complement of the other treatises of speculative philosophy, seen in retrospect, a science of rational order amongst sciences.

The "notions of logic" with which he introduces the other branches are, says the Cardinal, so plain that it is almost superfluous to enumerate them, "*tant elles sont de simple bon sens*," [1--"Traite Elfementaire de Philosophie," Vol. I, Introduction.] and he disposes of them in two pages of his textbook. Obviously this is not so simple when it comes to preparing the fallow ground of a girl's mind; but it gives some idea of the proportion to be observed in the use of this instrument at the outset, and may save both the teacher and the child from beguiling themselves to little purpose among the moods and figures of the syllogism. The preliminary notions of logic must be developed, extended, and supplemented through the whole course as necessity arises, just as they have been already anticipated through the preparatory work done in every elementary subject. This method is not strictly scientific nor in accordance with the full-grown course of philosophy; it only claims to have "_le simple bon sens_" in its favour, and the testimony of experience to prove that it is of use. And it cannot be said to be wholly out of rational order if it follows the normal development of a growing mind, and answers questions as they arise and call for solution. It may be a rustic way of learning the elements of philosophy, but it answers its purpose, and does not interfere with more scientific and complete methods which may come later in order of time.

The importance of the "discipline" of psychology

can scarcely be over-estimated. With that of ethics it gives to the minds of women that which they most need for the happy attainment of their destiny in any sphere of life and for the fulfilment of its obligations. They must know themselves and their own powers in order to exercise control and direction on the current of their lives. The complaint made of many women is that they are wanting in self-control, creatures of impulse, erratic, irresponsible, at the mercy of chance influences that assume control of their lives for the moment, subject to "nerves," carried away by emotional enthusiasm beyond all bounds, and using a blind tenacity of will to land themselves with the cause they have embraced in a dead-lock of absurdity.

Such is the complaint. It would seem more pardonable if this tendency to extremes and impulsiveness were owned to as a defect. But to be erratic is almost assumed as a pose. It is taken up as if self-discipline were dull, and control reduced vitality and killed the interest of life. The phase may not last, stronger counsels may prevail again. In a few years it may be hoped that this school of "impressionism" in conduct will be out of vogue, but for the moment it would seem as if its weakness and mobility, and restlessness were rather admired. It has created a kind of automobilism--if the word may be allowed--of mind and manners, an inclination to be perpetually "on the move," too much pressed for time to do anything at all, permanently unsettled, in fact to be *unsettled* is its habitual condition if not its recognized plan of life.

It is not contended that psychology and ethics would of themselves cure this tendency, but they would undoubtedly aid in doing so, for the confusion of wanting to do better and yet not knowing what to do is a most pathetic form of helplessness. A little knowledge of psychology would at least give an idea of the resources which the human soul has at its command when it seeks to take itself in hand. It would allow of some response to a reasonable appeal from outside. And all the time the first principles of ethics would refuse to be killed in the mind, and would continue to bear witness against the waste of existence and the diversion of life from its true end.

Rational principles of aesthetics belong very intimately to the education of women. Their ideas of beauty, their taste in art, influence very powerfully their own lives and those of others, and may transfigure many things which are otherwise liable to fall into the commonplace and the vulgar. If woman's taste is trained to choose the best, it upholds a standard which may save a generation from decadence. This concerns the beautiful and the fitting in all things where the power of art makes itself felt as "the expression of an ideal in a concrete work capable of producing an impression and attaching the beholder to that ideal which it presents for admiration." [1--Cardinal Mercier, "General Metaphysics," Part iv., Ch. iv.] It touches on all questions of taste, not only in the fine arts but in fiction, and furniture, and dress, and all the minor arts of life and adaptation of human skill to the external conditions of living. The importance of all these in their effect on the happiness and goodness of a whole people is a plea for not leaving out the principles of aesthetics, as well as the practice of some form of art from the education of girls.

The last and most glorious treatise in philosophy of which some knowledge can be given at the end of a school course is that of natural theology. If it is true, as they say, that St. Thomas Aquinas at the age of five years used to go round to the monks of Monte Cassino pulling them down by the sleeve to whisper his inquiry, "quid est Deus"? it may be hoped that older children are not incapable of appreciating some of the first notions that may be drawn from reason about the Creator, those truths "concerning the existence of God which are the supreme conclusion and crown of the department of physics, and those concerning His nature which apply the truths of general metaphysics to a determinate being, the Absolutely Perfect." [1--Cardinal Mercier, "Natural Theology," Introduction.] It is in the domain of natural theology that they will often find a safeguard against difficulties which may occur later in life, when they meet inquirers whose questions about God are not so ingenuous as that of the infant St. Thomas. The armour of their faith will not be so easily pierced by chance shots as if they were without preparation, and at the same time they will know enough of the greatness of the subject not to challenge "any unbeliever" to single combat, and undertake to prove against all opponents the existence and perfections of God.

For instruction as well as for defence the relation of philosophy to revealed truth should be explained. It is necessary to point out that while science has its own sphere within which it is independent, having its own principles and methods and means of certitude, [1--De Bonald and others were condemned and reproved by Gregory XVI for teaching that reason drew its first principles and grounds of certitude from revelation.] yet the Church as the guardian of revealed truth is obliged to prosecute for trespass those who in teaching any science encroach by affirmation or contradiction on the domain of revelation.

To sum up, therefore, logic can train the students to discriminate between good and bad arguments, which few ordinary readers can do, and not even every writer. Ethics teaches the rational basis of morals which it is useful for all to know, and psychology can teach to discriminate between the acts of intellect and will on the one hand and imagination and emotion on the other, and so furnish the key to many a puzzle of thought that has led to false and dangerous theorizing.

The method of giving instruction in the different branches of philosophy will depend so much on the preparation of the particular pupils, and also on the cast of mind of the teachers, that it is difficult to offer suggestions, except to point out this very fact that each mind needs to be met just where it is--with its own mental images, vocabulary, habit of thought and attention, all calling for consideration and adaptation of the subject to their particular case. It depends on the degree of preparation of the teachers to decide whether the form of a lecture is safest, or whether they can risk themselves in the arena of question and answer, the most useful in itself but requiring a far more complete training in preparation. If it can be obtained that the pupils state their own questions and difficulties in writing, a great deal will have been gained, for a good statement of a question is half-way to the right solution. If, after hearing a lecture or oral lesson, they can answer in writing Borne simple questions carefully stated, it will be a further advance. It is something to grasp accurately the scope of a question. The plague of girls' answers is usually irrelevancy from want of thought as to the scope of questions or even from inattention to their wording. If they can be patient in face of unanswered difficulties, and wait for the solution to come later on in its natural course, then at least one small fruit of their studies will have been brought to maturity; and if at the end of their elementary course they are convinced of their own ignorance, and want to know more, it may be said that the course has not been unsuccessful.

It is not, however, complete unless they know something of the history of philosophy, the great schools, and the names which have been held in honour from the beginning down to our own days. They will realize that it is good to have been born in their own time, and to learn such lessons now that the revival of scholastic philosophy under Leo XIII and the development of the neo-scholastic teaching have brought fresh life into the philosophy of tradition, which although it appears to put new wine into old bottles, seems able to preserve the wine and the bottles together.

CHAPTER V.

THE REALITIES OF LIFE.

"He fixed thee mid this dance Of plastic
circumstance, This Present, thou, forsooth, wouldst
fain arrest: Machinery just meant To give thy soul
its bent, Try thee and turn thee forth, sufficiently
impressed." BROWNING, "Rabbi Ben Ezra." "Eh,
Dieu! nous marchons trop en enfants--cela me
fache!" ST. JANE FRANCES DE CHANTAL.

One of the problems which beset school education,
and especially education in boarding schools, is the
difficulty of combining the good things it can give
with the best preparation for after life. This
preparation has to be made under circumstances
which necessarily keep children away from many of
the realities that have to be faced in the future.

To be a small member of a large organization has an
excellent effect upon the mind. From the presence
of numbers a certain dignity gathers round many
things that would in themselves be insignificant.
Ideas of corporate life with its obligations and
responsibilities are gained. Honoured traditions and
ideals are handed down if the school has a history
and spirit of its own. There are impressive and
solemn moments in the life of a large school which
remain in the memory as something beautiful and
great. The close of a year, with its retrospect and
anticipation, its restrained emotion from the pathos
which attends all endings and beginnings in life,
fills even the younger children with some transient
realization of the meaning of it all, and lifts them up

to a dim sense of the significance of existence, while for the elder ones such days leave engraven upon the mind thoughts which can never be effaced. These deep impressions belong especially to old-established schools, and are bound up with their past, with their traditional tone, and the aims that are specially theirs. In this they cannot be rivalled. The school-room at home is always the school-room, it has no higher moods, no sentiment of its own.

There are diversities of gifts for school and for home education; for impressiveness a large school has the advantage. It is also, in general, better off in the quality of its teachers, and it can turn their rifts to better account. A modern governess would require to be a host in herself to supply the varied demands of a girl's education, in the subjects to be taught, in companionship and personal influence, in the training of character, in watching over physical development, and even if she should possess in herself all that would be needed, there is the risk of "incompatibility of temperament" which makes a _tete-a-tete_ life in the school-room trying on both sides. School has the advantage of bringing the influence of many minds to bear, so that it is rare that a child should pass through a school course without coming in contact with some who awaken and understand and influence her for good. It offers too the chance of making friends, and though "sets" and cliques, plagues of school life, may give trouble and unsettle the weaker minds from time to time, yet if the current of the school is healthy it will set against them, and on the other hand the choicest and best friendships often begin and grow to maturity in the common life of school. The sodalities and congregations in Catholic schools are training grounds within the general system of training, in which higher ideals are aimed at, the obligation of using influence for good is pressed home, and the instincts of leadership turned to account for the common good. Lastly, among the advantages of school may be counted a general purpose and plan in the curriculum, and better appliances for methodical teaching than are usually available in private school-rooms, and where out-door games are in honour they add a great zest to school life.

But, as in all human things, there are drawbacks to school education, and because it is in the power of those who direct its organization to counteract some of these drawbacks, it is worth while to examine them and consider the possible remedies.

In the first place it will probably be agreed that boarding-school life is not desirable for very young children, as their well-being requires more elasticity in rule and occupations than is possible if they are together in numbers. Little children, out of control and excited, are a misery to themselves and to each other, and if they are kept in hand enough to protect the weaker ones from the exuberant energy of the stronger, then the strictness chafes them all, and spontaneity is too much checked. The informal play which is possible at home, with the opportunities for quiet and even solitude, are much better for young children than the atmosphere of school, though a day-school, with the hours of home life in between, is sometimes successfully adapted to their wants. But the special cases which justify parents in sending young children to boarding schools are numerous, now that established home life is growing more rare, and they have to be counted with in any large school. It can only be said that the yoke ought to be made as light as possible--short lessons, long sleep, very short intervals of real application of mind, as much open air as possible, bright rooms, and a mental atmosphere that tends to calm rather than to excite them. They should be saved from the petting of the elder girls, in whom this apparent kindness is often a selfish pleasure, bad on both sides.

For older children the difficulties are not quite the same, and instead of forcing them on too fast, school life may even keep them back. When children are assembled together in considerable numbers the intellectual level is that of the middle class of mind and does not favour the best, the outlook and conversation are those of the average, the language and vocabulary are on the same level, with a tendency to sink rather than to rise, and though emulation may urge on the leading spirits and keep them at racing speed, this does not quicken the interest in knowledge for its own sake, and the work is apt to slacken when the stimulus is withdrawn. And all the time there is comfort to the easy-going average in the consciousness of how many there are behind them.

The necessity for organization and foresight in detail among large numbers is also unfavourable to individual development. For children to find everything prepared for them, to feel no friction in the working of the machinery, so that all happens as it ought to, without effort and personal trouble on their part, to be told what to do, and only have to follow the bells for the ordering of their time--all this tends to diminish their resourcefulness and their patience with the unforeseen checks and cross-purposes and mistakes that they will have to put up with on leaving school. As a matter of fact the more perfect the school machinery, the smoother its working, the less does it prepare for the rutty road afterwards, and in this there is some consolation when school machinery jars from time to time in the working; if it teaches patience it is not altogether regrettable, and the little trouble which may arise in the material order is perhaps more educating than the regularity which has been disturbed.

We are beginning to believe what has never ceased to be said, that lessons in lesson-books are not the whole of education. The whole system of teaching in the elementary schools has been thrown off its balance by too many lesson-books, but it is righting itself again, and some of the memoranda on teaching, issued by the Board of Education within the last few years, are quite admirable in their practical suggestions for promoting a more efficient preparation for life. The Board now insists on the teaching of handicrafts, training of the senses in observation, development of knowledge, taste, and skill in various departments which are useful for life, and for girls especially on things which make the home. The same thing is wanted in middle-class education, though parents of the middle-class still look a little askance at household employments for their daughters. But children of the wealthier and upper classes take to them as a birthright, with the cordial assent of their parents and the applause of the doctors. It is for these children, so well-disposed for a practical education, and able to carry its influence so far, that we may consider what can be done in school life.

We ourselves who have to do with children must first appreciate the realities of life before we can communicate this understanding to others or give the right spirit to those we teach. And "the realities of life" may stand as a name for all those things which have to be learned in order to live, and which lesson-books do not teach. The realities of life are not material things, but they are very deeply wrought in with material things. There are things to be done, and things to be made, and things to be ordered and controlled, belonging to the primitive wants of human life, and to all those fundamental cares which have to support it. They are best learned in the actual doing from those who know how to do them; for although manuals and treatises exist for every possible department of skill and activity, yet the human voice and hand go much further in making knowledge acceptable than the textbook with diagrams. The dignity of manual labour comes home from seeing it well done, it is shown to be worth doing and deserving of honour.

Something which cannot be shown to children, but it will come to them later on as an inheritance, is the effect of manual work upon their whole being. Manual work gives balance and harmony in the development of the growing creature. A child does not attain its full power unless every faculty is exercised in turn, and to think that hard mental work alternated with hard physical exercise will give it full and wholesome development is to ignore whole provinces of its possessions. Generally speaking, children have to take the value of their mental work on the faith of our word. They must go through a great deal in mastering the rudiments of, say, Latin grammar (for the honey is not yet spread so thickly over this as it is now over the elements of modern languages). They must wonder why "grown-ups" have such an infatuation for things that seem out of place and inappropriate in life as they consider it worth living. Probably it is on this account that so many artificial rewards and inducements have had to be brought in to sustain their efforts. Physical exercise is a joy to healthy children, but it leaves nothing behind as a result. Children are proud of what they have done and made themselves. They lean upon the concrete, and to see as the result of their efforts something which lasts, especially something useful, as a witness to their power and skill, this is a reward in itself and needs no artificial stimulus, though to measure their own work in comparative excellence with that of others adds an element that quickens the desire to do well. Children will go quietly back again and again to look, without saying anything, at something they have made with their own hands, their eyes telling all that it means to them, beyond what they can express.

With its power of ministering to harmonious development of the faculties manual work has a direct influence on fitness for home and social life. It greatly develops good sense and aptitude for dealing with ordinary difficulties as they arise. In

common emergencies it is the "handy" member of
the household whose judgment and help are called
upon, not the brilliant person or one who has
specialized in any branch, but the one who can do
common things and can invent resources when
experience fails. When the specialist is at fault and
the artist waits for inspiration, the handy person
conies in and saves the situation, unprofessionally,
like the bone-setter, without much credit, but to the
great comfort of every one concerned.

Manual work likewise saves from eccentricity or
helps to correct it. Eccentricity may appear
harmless and even interesting, but in practice it is
found to be a drawback, enfeebling some sides of a
character, throwing the judgment at least on some
points out of focus. In children it ought to be
recognized as a defect to be counteracted. When
people have an overmastering genius which of itself
marks out for them a special way of excellence,
some degree of eccentricity is easily pardoned, and
almost allowable. But eccentricity unaccompanied
by genius is mere uncorrected selfishness, or want
of mental balance. It is selfishness if it could be
corrected and is not, because it makes exactions
from others without return. It will not adapt itself to
them but insists on being taken as it is, whether
acceptable or not. At best, eccentricity is a morbid
tendency liable to run into extremes when its habits
are undisturbed. An excuse sometimes made for
eccentricity is that it is a security against any further
mental aberration, perhaps on the same principle
that inoculation producing a mild form of diseases
is sometimes a safeguard against their attacks. But
if the mind and habits of life can be brought under

control, so as to take part in ordinary affairs without attracting attention or having exemptions and allowance made for them, a result of a far higher order will have been attained. To recognize eccentricity as selfishness is a first step to its cure, and to make oneself serviceable to others is the simplest corrective. Whatever else they may be, "eccentrics" are not generally serviceable.

Children of vivid imagination, nervously excitable and fragile in constitution, rather easily fall into little eccentric ways which grow very rapidly and are hard to overcome. One of the commonest of these is talking to themselves. Sitting still, making efforts to apply their minds to lessons for more than a short time, accentuates the tendency by nerve fatigue. In reaction against fatigue the mind falls into a vacant state and that is the best condition for the growth of eccentricities and other mental troubles. If their attention is diverted from themselves, and yet fixed with the less exhausting concentration which belongs to manual work, this diversion into another channel, with its accompany bodily movement, will restore the normal balance, and the little eccentric pose will be forgotten; this is better than being noticed and laughed at and formally corrected.

Manual employments, especially if varied, and household occupations afford a great variety, give to children a sense of power in knowing what to do in a number of circumstances; they take pleasure in this, for it is a thing which they admire in others. Domestic occupations also form in them a habit of decision, from the necessity of getting through things which will not wait. For domestic duties do not allow of waiting for a moment of inspiration or delaying until a mood of depression or indifference has passed. They have a quiet, imperious way of commanding, and an automatic system of punishing when they are neglected, which are more convincing that exhortations. Perhaps in this particular point lies their saving influence against nerves and moodiness and the demoralization of "giving way." Those who have no obligations, whose work will wait for their convenience, and who can if they please let everything go for a time, are more easily broken down by trouble than those whose household duties still have to be done, in the midst of sorrow and trial. There is something in homely material duties which heals and calms the mind and gives it power to come back to itself. And in sudden calamities those who know how to make use of their hands do not helplessly wring them, or make trouble worse by clinging to others for support.

Again, circumstances sometimes arise in school life which make light household duties an untold boon for particular children. Accidental causes, troubles of eyesight, or too rapid growth, etc., may make regular study for a time impossible to them. These children become *exempt* persons, and even if they are able to take some part in the class work the time of preparation is heavy on their hands. Exempt persons easily develop undesirable qualities, and their apparent privileges are liable to unsettle others. As a matter of fact those who are able to keep the common life have the best of it, but they are apt to look upon the exemption of others as enviable, as they long for gipsy life when a caravan passes by. With the resource of household employment to give occupation it becomes apparent that exemption does not mean holiday, but the substitution of one duty or lesson for another, and this is a principle which holds good in after life-- that except in case of real illness no one is justified in having nothing to do.

Lastly, the work of the body is good for the soul, it drives out silliness as effectually as the rod, since that which was of old considered as the instrument for exterminating the "folly bound up in the heart of a child," has been laid aside in the education of girls. It is a great weapon against the seven devils of whom one is Sloth and another Pride, and it prepares a sane mind in a sound body for the discipline of after life.

Experience bears its own testimony to the failure of an education which is out of touch with the material requirements of life. It leaves an incomplete power of expression, and some dead points in the mind from which no response can be awakened. To taste of many experiences seems to be necessary for complete development. When on the material side all is provided without forethought, and people are exempt from all care and obligation, a whole side of development is wanting, and on that side the mind remains childish, inexperienced, and unreal. The best mental development is accomplished under the stress of many demands. One claim balances the other; a touch of hardness and privation gives strength of mind and makes self-denial a reality; a little anxiety teaches foresight and draws out resourcefulness, and the tendency to fret about trifles is corrected by the contact of the realities of life.

To come to practice--What can be done for girls during their years at school?

In the first place the teaching of the fundamental handicraft of women, needlework, deserves a place of honour. In many schools it has almost perished by neglect, or the thorns of the examination programme have grown up and choked it. This misfortune has been fairly common where the English "University Locals" and the Irish "Intermediate" held sway. There literally was not time for it, and the loss became so general that it was taken as a matter of course, scarcely regretted; to the children themselves, so easily carried off by *vogue*, it became almost a matter for self-complacency, "not to be able to hold a needle" was accepted as an indication of something superior in attainments. And it must be owned that there were certain antiquated methods of teaching the art which made it quite excusable to "hate needlework." One "went through so much to learn so little"; and the results depending so often upon help from others to bring them to any conclusion, there was no sense of personal achievement in a work accomplished. Others planned, cut out and prepared the work, and the child came in as an unwilling and imperfect sewing machine merely to put in the stitches. The sense of mastery over material was not developed, yet that is the only way in which a child's attainment of skill can be linked on to the future. What cannot be done without help always at hand drops out of life, and likewise that which calls for no application of mind.

To reach independence in the practical arts of life is an aim that will awaken interests and keep up efforts, and teachers have only a right to be satisfied when their pupils can do without them. This is not the finishing point of a course of teaching, it is a whole system, beginning in the first steps and continuing progressively to the end. It entails upon teachers much labour, much thought, and the sacrifice of showy results. The first look of finish depends more upon the help of the teacher than upon the efforts of children. Their results must be waited for, and they will in the early years have a humbler, more rough-hewn look than those in which expert help has been given. But the educational advantages are not to be compared.

A four years' course, two hours per week, gives a thorough grounding in plain needlework, and girls are then capable of beginning dressmaking, in they can reach a very reasonable proficiency when they leave school. Whether they turn this to practical account in their own homes, or make use of it in Clothing Societies and Needlework Guilds for the poor, the knowledge is of real value. If fortune deals hardly with them, and they are thrown on their own resources later in life, it is evident that to make their own clothes is a form of independence for which they will be very thankful. Another branch of needlework that ought to form part of every Catholic girl's education is that of work for the Church in which there is room for every capacity, from the hemming of the humblest *lavabo* towel to priceless works of art embroidered by queens for the popes and bishops of their time.

"First aid," and a few practical principles of nursing, can sometimes be profitably taught in school, if time is made for a few lessons, perhaps during one term. The difficulty of finding time even adds to the educational value, since the conditions of life outside do not admit of uniform intervals between two bells. Enough can be taught to make girls able to take their share helpfully in cases of illness in their homes, and it is a branch of usefulness in which a few sensible notions go a long way.

General self-help is difficult to define or describe, but it can be taught at school more than would appear at first sight, if only those engaged in the education of children will bear in mind that the triumph of their devotedness is to enable children to do without them. This is much more laborious than to do things efficiently and admirably for them, but it is real education. They can be taught as mothers would teach them at home, to mend and keep their things in order, to prepare for journeys, pack their own boxes, be responsible for their labels and keys, write orders to shops, to make their own beds, dust their private rooms, and many other things which will readily occur to those who have seen the pitiful sight of girls unable to do them.

Finally, simple and elementary cooking comes well within the scope of the education of elder girls at school. But it must be taught seriously to make it worth while, and as in the teaching of needlework,

the foundations must be plain. To begin by fancy-
work in one case and bonbons in the other turns the
whole instruction into a farce. In this subject
especially, the satisfaction of producing good work,
well done, without help, is a result which justifies
all the trouble that may be spent upon it. When girls
have, by themselves, brought to a happy conclusion
the preparation of a complete meal, their very faces
bear witness to the educational value of the success.
They are not elated nor excited, but wear the look of
quiet contentment which seems to come from
contact with primitive things. This look alone on a
girl's face gives a beauty of its own, something
becoming, and fitting, and full of promise. No
expression is equal to it in the truest charm, for
quiet contentment is the atmosphere which in the
future, whatever may be her lot, ought to be
diffused by her presence, an atmosphere of security
and rest.

Perhaps at first sight it seems an exaggeration to
link so closely together the highest natural graces of
a woman with those lowliest occupations, but let
the effects be compared by those who have
examined other systems of instruction. If they have
considered the outcome of an exclusively
intellectual education for girls, especially one
loaded with subjects in sections to be "got up" for
purposes of examination, and compared it with one
into which the practical has largely entered, they
can hardly fail to agree that the latter is the best
preparation for life, not only physically and morally
but mentally. During the stress of examinations
lined foreheads, tired eyes, shallow breathing,
angular movements tell their own story of strain,

and when it is over a want of resourcefulness in finding occupation shows that a whole side has remained undeveloped. The possibility of turning to some household employments would give rest without idleness; it would save from two excesses in a time of reaction, from the exceeding weariness of having nothing to do, the real misery of an idle life, and on the other hand from craving for excitement and constant change through fear of this unoccupied vacancy.

One other point is worth consideration. The "servant question" is one which looms larger and larger as a household difficulty. There are stories of great and even royal households being left in critical moments at the mercy of servants' tempers, of head cooks "on strike" or negligent personal attendants. And from these down to the humblest employers of a general servant the complaint is the same--servants so independent, so exacting, good servants not to be had, so difficult to get things properly done, etc. These complaints give very strong warning that helpless dependence on servants is too great a risk to be accepted, and that every one in ordinary stations of life should be at least able to be independent of personal service. The expansion of colonial life points in the same direction. The "simple life" is talked of at home, but it is really lived in the colonies. Those who brace themselves to its hardness find a vigour and resourcefulness within them which they had never suspected, and the pride of personal achievement in making a home brings out possibilities which in softer circumstances might have remained for ever dormant, with their treasure of happiness and hardy virtues. It is possible, no doubt, in that severe and plain life to lose many things which are not replaced by its self-reliance and hardihood. It is possible to drop into merely material preoccupation in the struggle for existence. But it is also possible not to do so, and the difference lies in having an ideal.

To Catholics even work in the wilderness and life in the backwoods are not dissociated from the most spiritual ideals. The pioneers of the Church, St. Benedict's monks, have gone before in the very same labour of civilization when Europe was to a great extent still in backwoods. And, when they sanctified their days in prayer and hard labour, poetry did not forsake them, and learning even took refuge with them in their solitude to wait for better times. It was religion which attracted both. Without their daily service of prayer, the *Opus Dei*, and the assiduous copying of books, and the desire to build worthy churches for the worship of God, arts and learning would not have followed the monks into the wilderness, but their life would have dropped to the dead level of the squatter's existence. In the same way family life, if toilsome, either at home or in a new country, may be inspired by the example of the Holy Family in Nazareth; and in lonely and hard conditions, as well as in the stress of our crowded ways of living, the influence of that ideal reaches down to the foundations and transfigures the very humblest service of the household.

These primitive services which are at the foundation of all home life are in themselves the same in all places and times. There is in them something almost sacred; they are sane, wholesome, stable, amid the weary perpetual change of artificial additions which add much to the cares but little to the joys of life. There is a long distance between the labours of Benedictine monks and the domestic work possible for school girls, but the principles fundamental to both are the same--happiness in willing work, honour to manual labour, service of God in humble offices. The work of lay-sisters in some religious houses, where they understand the happiness of their lot, links the two extremes together across the centuries. The jubilant onset of their company in some laborious work is like an anthem rising to God, bearing witness to the happiness of labour where it is part of His service. They are the envy of the choir religious, and in the precincts of such religious houses children unconsciously learn the dignity of manual labour, and feel themselves honoured by having any share in it. Such labour can be had for love, but not for money.

One word must be added before leaving the subject of the realities of life. Worn time to time a rather emphatic school lifts up its voice in the name of plain speaking and asks for something beyond reality--for realism, for anticipated instruction on the duties and especially on the dangers of grown-up life. It will be sufficient to suggest three points for consideration in this matter: (1) That these demands are not made by fathers and mothers, but appear to come from those whose interest in children is indirect and not immediately or personally responsible. This may be supposed from the fact that they find fault with what is omitted, but do not give their personal experience of how the want may be supplied. (2) Those priests who have made a special study of children do not seem to favour the view, or to urge that any change should be made in the direction of plain speaking. (3) The answer given by a great educational authority, Miss Dorothea Beale, the late Principal of Cheltenham College, may appeal to those who are struck by the theory if they do not advocate it in practice. When this difficulty was laid before her she was not in favour of departing from the usual course, or insisting on the knowledge of grown-up life before its time, and she pointed out that in case of accidents or surgical operations it was not the doctors nor the nurses actively engaged who turned faint and sick, but those who had nothing to do, and in the same way she thought that such instruction, cut off from the duties and needs of the present, was not likely to be of any real benefit, but rather to be harmful. Considering how wide was her experience of educational work this opinion carries great weight.

CHAPTER VI.

LESSONS AND PLAY.

"What think we of thy soul?

"Born of full stature, lineal to control; And yet a pigmy's yoke must undergo. Yet must keep pace and tarry, patient, kind, With its unwilling scholar, the dull, tardy mind; Must be obsequious to the body's powers, Whose low hands mete its paths, set ope and close its ways, Must do obeisance to the days, And wait the little pleasure of the hours; Yea, ripe for kingship, yet must be Captive in statuted minority!" "Sister Songs," by FRANCIS THOMPSON.

Lessons and play used to be as clearly marked off one from the other as land and water on the older maps. Now we see some contour maps in which the land below so many feet and the sea within so many fathoms' depth are represented by the same marking, or left blank. In the same way the tendency in education at present is almost to obliterate the line of demarcation, at least for younger children, so that lessons become a particular form of play, "with a purpose," and play becomes a sublimated form of lessons, as the druggists used to say, "an elegant preparation" of something bitter. If the Board of Education were to name a commission composed of children, and require it to look into the system, it is doubtful whether they would give a completely satisfactory report. They would probably judge it to be too uniform in tone, poor in colour and contrast, deficient in sparkle. They like the exhilaration of bright colour, and the crispness of contrast. Of course they would judge it from the standpoint of play, not of lessons. But play which is not quite play, coming after something which has been not quite lessons, loses the tingling delight of contrast. The funereal tolling of a bell for real lessons made a dark background against which the rapture of release for real play shone out with a brilliancy which more than made up for it. At home, the system of ten minutes' lessons at short intervals seems to answer well for young children; it exerts just enough pressure to give rebound in the intervals of play. Of course this is not possible at school.

But the illusion that lessons are play cannot be indefinitely kept up, or if the illusion remains it is fraught with trouble. Duty and endurance, the power to go through drudgery, the strength of mind to persist in taking trouble, even where no interest is felt, the satisfaction of holding on to the end in doing something arduous, these things must be learned at some time during the years of education. If they are not learned then, in all probability they will never be acquired at all; examples to prove the contrary are rare. The question is how--and when. If pressed too soon with obligations of lessons, especially with prolonged attention, little anxious faces and round shoulders protest. If too long delayed the discovery comes as a shock, and the less energetic fall out at once and declare that they "can't learn"--"never could."

Perhaps in one way the elementary schools with their large classes have a certain advantage in this, because the pressure is more self-adjusting than in higher class education, where the smaller numbers give to each child a greater share in the general work, for better or for worse. In home education this share becomes even greater when sometimes one child alone enjoys or endures the undivided attention of the governess. In that case the pressure does not relax. But out of large classes of infants in elementary schools it is easy to see on many vacant restful faces that after a short exertion in "qualifying to their teacher" they are taking their well-earned rest. They do not allow themselves to be strung up to the highest pitch of attention all through the lesson, but take and leave as they will or as they can, and so they are carried through a fairly long period of lessons without distress. As they grow older and more independent in their work the same cause operates in a different way. They can go on by themselves and to a certain extent they must do so, as o n account of the numbers teachers can give less time and less individual help to each, and the habit of self-reliance is gradually acquired, with a certain amount of drudgery, leading to results proportionate to the teacher's personal power of stimulating work. The old race of Scottish schoolmaster in the rural schools produced--perhaps still produces--good types of such self-reliant scholars, urged on by his personal enthusiasm for knowledge. Having no assistant, his own personality was the soul of the school, both boys and girls responding in a spirit which was worthy of it. But the boys had the best of it; "lassies" were not deemed worthy to touch the classics, and the classics were everything to him. In America it is reported that the best specimens of university students often come from remote schools in which no external advantages have been available; but the tough unyielding habit of study has been developed in grappling with difficulties without much support from a teacher.

With those who are more gently brought up the problem is how to obtain this habit of independent work, that is practically--how to get the will to act. There is drudgery to be gone through, however it may be disguised, and as a permanent acquisition the power of going through it is one of the most lasting educational results that can be looked for. Drudgery is labour with toil and fatigue. It is the long penitential exercise of the whole human race, not limited to one class or occupation, but accompanying every work of man from the lowest mechanical factory hand or domestic "drudge" up to the Sovereign Pontiff, who has to spend so many hours in merely receiving, encouraging, blessing, and dismissing the unending processions of his people as they pass before him, imparting to them graces of which he can never see the fruit, and then returning to longer hours of listening to complaints and hearing of troubles which often admit of no remedy: truly a life of labour with toil and fatigue, in comparison with which most lives are easy, though each has to bear in its measure the same stamp. Pius X has borne the yoke of labour from his youth. His predecessor took it up with an enthusiasm that burned within him, and accepted training in a service where the drudgery is as severe though generally kept out of sight. The acceptance of it is the great matter, whatever may be the form it takes.

Spurs and bait, punishment and reward, have been used from time immemorial to set the will in motion, and the results have been variable--no one has appeared to be thoroughly satisfied with either, or even with a combination of the two. Some authorities have stood on an eminence, and said that neither punishment nor reward should be used, that knowledge should be loved for its own sake. But if it was not loved, after many invitations, the problem remained. As usual the real solution seems to be attainable only by one who really loves both knowledge and children, or one who loves knowledge and can love children, as Vittorino da Feltre loved them both, and also Blessed Thomas More. These two affections mingled together produce great educators--great in the proportion in which the two are possessed--as either one or the other declines the educational power diminishes, till it dwindles down to offer trained substitutes and presentable mediocrities for living teachers. The fundamental principle reasserts itself, that "love feels no labour, or if it does it loves the labour."

Here is one of our Catholic secrets of strength. We have received so much, we have so much to give, we know so well what we want to obtain. We have the Church, the great teacher of the world, as our prototype, and by some instinct a certain unconscious imitation of her finds its way into the mind and heart of Catholic teachers, so that, though often out of poorer material, we can produce teachers who excel in personal hold over children, and influence for good by their great affection and the value which they set on souls. Their power of obtaining work is proportioned to their own love of knowledge, and here--let it be owned--we more often fail. Various theories are offered in explanation of this; people take one or other according to their personal point of view. Some say we feel so sure of the other world that our hold on this is slack. Some that in these countries we have not yet made up for the check of three centuries when education was made almost impossible for us. And others say it is not true at all. Perhaps they know best.

Next to the personal power of the teacher to influence children in learning lessons comes an essential condition to make it possible, and that is a simple life with quiet regular hours and unexciting pleasures. Amid a round of amusements lessons must go to the wall, no child can stand the demands of both at a time. All that can be asked of them is that they should live through the excitement without too much weariness or serious damage. The place to consider this is in London at the children's hour for riding in the park, contrasting the prime condition of the ponies with the "illustrious pallor" of so many of their riders. They have courage enough left to sit up straight in their saddles, but it would take a heart of stone to think of lesson books. This extreme of artificial life is of course the portion of the few. Those few, however, are very important people, influential in the future for good or evil, but a protest from a distance would not reach their schoolrooms, any more than legislation for the protection of children; they may be protected from work, but not from amusement. The conditions of simple living which are favourable for children have been so often enumerated that it is unnecessary to go over them again; they may even be procured in tabular form or graphical representation for those to whom these figures and curves carry conviction.

But a point that is of more practical interest to children and teachers, struggling together in the business of education, and one that is often overlooked, is that children do not know how to learn lessons when the books are before them, and that there is a great waste of good power, and a great deal of unnecessary weariness from this cause. If the cause of imperfectly learned lessons is examined it will usually be found there, and also the cause of so much dislike to the work of preparation. Children do not know by instinct how to set about learning a lesson from a book, nor do they spontaneously recognize that there are different ways of learning, adapted to different lessons. It is a help to them to know that there is one way for the multiplication table and another for history and another for poetry, as the end of the lesson is different. They can understand this if it is put before them that one is learnt most quickly by mere repetition, until it becomes a sing-song in the memory that cannot go wrong, and that afterwards in practice it will allow itself to be taken to pieces; they will see that they can grasp a chapter of history more intelligently if they prepare for themselves questions upon it which might be asked of another, than in trying by mechanical devices of memory to associate facts with something to hold them by; that poetry is different from both, having a body and a soul, each of which has to be taken account of in learning it, one of them being the song and the other the singer. Obviously there is not one only way for each of these or for other matters which have to be learnt, but one of the greatest difficulties is removed when it is understood that there is something intelligible to be done in the learning of lessons beyond reading them over and over with the hope that they will go in.

The hearing of lessons is a subject that deserves a great deal of consideration. It is an old formal name for what has been often an antiquated mechanical exercise. A great deal more trouble is expended now on the manner of questioning and "hearing" the lessons; but even yet it may be done too formally, as a mere function, or in a way that kills the interest, or in a manner that alarms--with a mysterious face as if setting traps, or with questions that are easy and obvious to ask, but for children almost impossible to answer. Children do not usually give direct answers to simple questions. Experience seems to have taught them that appearances are deceptive in this matter, and they look about for the spring by which the trap works before they will touch the bait. It is a pity to set traps, because it destroys confidence, and children's confidence in such matters as lessons is hard to win.

The question of aids to study by stimulants is a difficult one. On the one hand it seems to some educators a fundamental law that reward should follow right-doing and effort, and so no doubt it is; but the reward within one's own mind and soul is one thing and the calf-bound book is another-- scarcely even a symbol of the first, because they are not always obtained by the same students. This is a fruitful subject for discourse or reflection at distributions of prizes. Those who are behind the scenes know that the race is not to the swift nor the battle to the strong, and the children know it themselves, and prize-winners often become the object of the "word in season," pointing out how rarely they will be found to distinguish themselves in after life; while the steady advance of the plodding and slow mind is dwelt upon, and those who have failed through idleness drink up the encouragement which was not intended for them, and feel that they are the hope of the future because they have won no prizes. It is difficult on those occasions to make the conflicting conclusions clear to everybody.

Yet the system of prize distributions is time honoured and traditional, and every country is not yet so disinterested in study as to be able to do without it; under its sway a great deal of honest effort is put out, and the taste of success which is the great stimulant of youth is first experienced.

There is also the system of certificates, which has the advantage of being open to many instead of to one. It is likewise a less material testimonial, approaching more nearly to the merited word of approval which is in itself the highest human reward, and the one nearest to the heart of things, because it is the one which belongs to home. For if the home authorities interest themselves in lessons at all, their grown-up standard and the paramount weight of their opinion gives to one word of their praise a dignity and worth which goes beyond all prizes. Beyond this there is no natural satisfaction to equal the inner consciousness of having done one's best, a very intimate prize distribution in which we ourselves make the discourse, and deliver the certificate to ourselves. This is the culminating point at which educators aim; they are all agreed that prizes in the end are meant to lead up to it, but the way is long between them. And both one and the other are good in so far as they lead us on to the highest judgment that is day by day passed on our work. When prizes, and even the honour of well-deserved praise, fail to attract, the thought of God the witness of our efforts, and of the value in His sight of striving which is never destined to meet with success, is a support that keeps up endurance, and seals with an evident mark of privilege the lives of many who have made those dutiful efforts not for themselves but in the sight of God.

The subject of play has to be considered from two points of view, that of the children and ours. Theirs is concerned chiefly with the present and ours with the future, far although we do not want every play-hour to be haunted with a spectral presence that speaks of improvement and advancement, yet we cannot lose sight of the fact that every hour of play is telling on the future, deepening the mark of the character, strengthening the habits, and guiding the lines of after life into this or that channel.

Looking at it from this point of view of the future, there seems to be something radically wrong at present with the play provided for children of nursery age. In a very few years we shall surely look back and wonder how we could have endured, for the children, the perverse reign of the Golliwog dynasty and the despotism of Teddy-bears. More than that, it is pitiful to hear of nurseries for Catholic children sometimes without shrine or altar or picture of the Mother of God, and with one of these monsters on every chair. Something even deeper than the artistic sense must revolt before long against this barbarous rule. The Teddy-bear, if he has anything to impart, suggests his own methods of life and defence, and the Golliwog, far worse--limp, hideous, without one characteristic grace, or spark of humour--suggests the last extremity of what is embodied in the expression "letting oneself go." And these things are loved! Pity the beautiful soul of the child, made for beautiful things. *Il y a toujours en nous quelque chose qui veut ramper*, said Pere de Ravignan, and to this the Golliwog makes strong appeal. It is only too easy to *let go*, and the Golliwog playfellow says that it is quite right to do so--he does it himself. It takes a great deal to make him able to sit up at all-- only in the most comfortable chair can it be accomplished--if the least obstacle is encountered he can only give way. And yet this pitiable being makes no appeal to the spirit of helpfulness. Do what you can for him it is impossible to raise him up, the only thing is to go down with him to his own level and stay there. The Golliwog is at heart a pessimist.

In contrast with this the presence of an altar or nursery shrine, though not a plaything, gives a different tone to play--a tone of joy and heavenliness that go down into the soul and take root there to grow into something lasting and beautiful. There are flowers to be brought, and lights, and small processions, and evening recollection with quietness of devotion, with security in the sense of heavenly protection, with the realization of the "great cloud of witnesses" who are around to make play safe and holy, and there is through it all the gracious call to things higher, to be strong, to be unselfish, to be self-controlled, to be worthy of these protectors and friends in heaven.

There is another side also to the question of nursery play, and that is what may be called the play-values of the things provided. Mechanical toys are wonderful, but beyond an artificial interest which comes mostly from the elders, there is very little lasting delight in them for children. They belong to the system of over-indulgence and over-stimulation which measures the value of things by their price. Their worst fault is that they do all there is to be done, while the child looks on and has nothing to do. The train or motor rushes round and round, the doll struts about and bleats "papa," "mama," the Teddy-bear growls and dances, and the owner has but to wind them up, which is very poor amusement. Probably they are better after they have been over-wound and the mechanical part has given way, and they have come to the hard use that belongs to their proper position as playthings. If a distinction may be drawn between toys and playthings, toys are of very little play-value, they stand for fancy play, to be fiddled with; while playthings stand as symbols of real life, the harder and more primitive side of life taking the highest rank, and all that they do is really done by the child. This is the real play-value. Even things that are not playthings at all, sticks and stones and shells, have this possibility in them. Things which have been found have a history of their own, which gives them precedence over what comes from a shop; but the highest value of all belongs to the things which children have made entirely themselves--bows and arrows, catapults, clay marbles, though imperfectly round, home-made boats and kites. The play-value grows in direct proportion to the amount of personal share which children have in the making and in the use of their playthings. And in this we ought cordially to agree with them.

After the nursery age, in the school or school-room, play divides into two lines--organized games, of which we hear a great deal in school at present, and home play. They are not at all the same thing. Both have something in their favour. So much has been written of late about the value of organized games, how they bring out unselfishness, prompt and unquestioning obedience, playing for one's side and not for oneself, etc., that it seems as if all has been said better than it could be said again, except perhaps to point out that there is little relaxation in the battle of life for children who do their best at books indoors and at games out of doors--so that in self-defence a good many choose an "elective course" between the two lines of advantages that school offers, and do not attempt to serve two masters; they will do well at books or games, but not at both. If the interest in games is keen, they require a great deal of will-energy, as well as physical activity, a great deal of self-control and subordination of personal interest to the good of the whole. In return for these requirements they give a great deal, this or that, more or less, according to the character of the game; they give physical control of movement, quickness of eye and hand, promptitude in decision, observance of right moments, command of temper, and many other things. In fact, for some games the only adverse criticism to offer is that they are more of a discipline than real play, and that certainly for younger children who have no other form of recreation than play, something more restful to the mind and less definite in purpose is desirable.

For these during playtime some semblance of solitude is exceedingly desirable at school where the great want is to be sometimes alone. It is good for them not to be always under the pressure of competition--going along a made road to a definite end--but to have their little moments of even comparative solitude, little times of silence and complete freedom, if they cannot be by themselves. Hoops and skipping-ropes without races or counted competitions will give this, with the possibility of a moment or two to do nothing but live and breathe and rejoice in air and sunshine. Without these moments of rest the conditions of life at present and the constitutions for which the new word "nervy" has had to be invented, will give us tempers and temperaments incapable of repose and solitude. A child alone in a swing, kicking itself backwards and forwards, is at rest; alone in its little garden it has complete rest of mind with the joy of seeing its own plants grow; alone in a field picking wild flowers it is as near to the heart of primitive existence as it is possible to be. Although these joys of solitude are only attainable in their perfection by children at home, yet if their value is understood, those who have charge of them at school can do something to give them breathing spaces free from the pressure of corporate life, and will probably find them much calmer and more manageable than if they have nothing but organized play.

There are plenty of indoor occupations too for little girls which may give the same taste of solitude and silence, approaching to those simpler forms of home play which have no definite aim, no beginning and ending, no rules. The fighting instinct is very near the surface in ambitious and energetic children, and in the play-grounds it asserts itself all the more in reaction after indoor discipline, then excitement grows, and the weaker suffer, and the stronger are exasperated by friction. If unselfish, they feel the effort to control themselves; if selfish, they exhaust themselves and others in the battle to impose their own will. In these moods solitude and silence, with a hoop or skipping-rope, are a saving system, and restore calmness of mind. All that is wanted is freedom, fresh air, and spontaneous movement. This is more evident in the case of younger children, but if it can be obtained for elder girls it is just as great a relief. They have usually acquired more self-control, and the need does not assert itself so loudly, but it is perhaps all the greater; and in whatever way it can best be ministered to, it will repay attention and the provision that may be made for it.

One word may be merely suggested for consideration concerning games in girls' schools, and that is the comparative value of them as to physical development. The influence of the game in vogue in each country will always be felt, but it is worth attention that some games, as hockey, conduce to all the attitudes and movements which are least to be desired, and that others, as basket-ball, on the contrary tend--if played with strict regard to rules--to attitudes which are in themselves beautiful and tending to grace of movement. This word belongs to our side of the question, not that of the children. It belongs to our side also to see that hoops are large, and driven with a stick, not a hook, for the sake of straight backs, which are so easily bent crooked in driving a small hoop with a hook.

In connexion with movement comes the question of dancing. Dancing comes, officially, under the heading of lessons, most earnest lessons if the professor has profound convictions of its significance. But dancing belongs afterwards to the playtime of life. We have outlived the grim puritanical prejudice which condemned it as wrong, and it is generally agreed that there is almost a natural need for dancing as the expression of something very deep in human nature, which seems to be demonstrated by its appearance in one form or another, amongst all races of mankind. There is something in co-ordinated rhythmical movement, in the grace of steps, in the buoyancy of beautiful dancing which seems to make it a very perfect exercise for children and young people. But there are dances and dances, steps and steps, and about the really beautiful there is always a touch of the severe, and a hint of the ideal. Without these, dancing drops at once to the level of the commonplace and below it. In general, dances which embody some characteristics of a national life have more beauty than cosmopolitan dances, but they are only seen in their perfection when performed by dancers of the race to whom their spirit belongs, or by the class for whom they are intended: which is meant as a suggestion that little girls should not dance the hornpipe.

In conclusion, the question of play, and playtime and recreation is absorbing more and more attention in grown-up life. We have heard it said over and over again of late years that we tire a nation at play, and that "the athletic craze" has gone beyond all bounds. Many facts are brought forward in support of this criticism from schools, from newspapers, from general surveys of our national life at present. And those who study more closely the Catholic body say that we too are sharing in this extreme, and that the Catholic body though small in number is more responsible and more deserving of reproof if it falls from its ideals, for it has ideals. It is only Catholic girls who concern us here, but our girls among other girls, and Catholic women among other women have the privilege as well as the duty of upholding what is highest. We belong by right to the graver side of the human race, for those who know must be in an emergency graver, less reckless on the one hand, less panic-stricken on the other, than those who do not know. We can never be entirely "at play." And if some of us should be for a time carried away by the current, and momentarily completely "at play," it must be in a wave of reaction from the long grinding of endurance under the penal times. Cardinal Newman's reminiscences of the life and ways of "the Roman Catholics" in his youth showy the temper of mind against which our present excess of play is a reaction.

"A few adherents of the Old Religion, moving
silently and sorrowfully about, as memorials of
what had been. 'The Roman Catholics'--not a sect,
not even an interest, as men conceived of it--not a
body, however small, representative of the Great
Communion abroad, but a mere handful of
individuals, who might be counted, like the pebbles
and detritus of the great deluge, and who, forsooth,
merely happened to retain a creed which, in its day
indeed, was the profession of a Church. Here a set
of poor Irishmen, coining and going at harvest time,
or a colony of them lodged in a miserable quarter of
the vast metropolis. There, perhaps, an elderly
person, seen walking in the streets, grave and
solitary, and strange, though noble in bearing, and
said to be of good family, and 'a Roman Catholic.'
An old-fashioned house of gloomy appearance,
closed in with high walls, with an iron gate, and
yews, and the report attaching to it that 'Roman
Catholics' lived there; but who they were, or what
they did, or what was meant by calling them Roman
Catholics, no one could tell, though it had an
unpleasant sound, and told of form and superstition.
And then, perhaps, as we went to and fro, looking
with a boy's curious eyes through the great city, we
might come to-day upon some Moravian chapel, or
Quaker's meeting-house, and to-morrow on a chapel
of the 'Roman Catholics': but nothing was to be
gathered from it, except that there were lights
burning there, and some boys in white, swinging
censers: and what it all meant could only be learned
from books, from Protestant histories and sermons;
but they did not report well of the 'Roman

Catholics,' but, on the contrary, deposed that they had once had power and had abused it. ... Such were the Catholics in England, found in corners, and alleys, and cellars, and the housetops, or in the recesses of the country; cut off from the populous world around them, and dimly seen, as if through a mist or in twilight, as ghosts flitting to and fro, by the high Protestants, the lords of the earth." ("The Second Spring.")

This it is from which we are keeping holiday; but for us it can be only a half holiday, the sifting process is always at work, the opposition of the world to the Church only sleeps for a moment, and there are many who tell us that the signs of the times point to new forms of older conflicts likely to recur, and that we may have to go, as they went on the day of Waterloo, straight from the dance to the battlefield.

CHAPTER VII.

MATHEMATICS, NATURAL SCIENCE, AND NATURE STUDY.

"The Arab told me that the stone (To give it in the language of the dream) Was "Euclid's Elements"; and "This," said he, "Is something of more worth"; and at the word Stretched forth the shell, so beautiful in shape, In colour so resplendent, with command That I should hold it to my ear. I did so, And heard that instant in an unknown tongue, Which yet I understood, articulate sounds, A loud prophetic blast of harmony." WORDSWORTH, "The Prelude," Bk. V.

Mathematics, natural science, and nature study may be conveniently grouped together, because in a study of educational aims, in so far as they concern Catholic girls, there is not much that is distinctive which practically affects these branches; during the years of school life they stand, more or less, on common ground with others. More advanced studies of natural science open up burning questions, and as to these, it is the last counsel of wisdom for girls leaving school or school-room to remember that they have no right to have any opinion at all. It is well to make them understand that after years of specialized study the really great men of science, in very gentle tones and with careful utterance, give to the world their formed opinions, keeping them ever open to readjustment as the results of fresh observations come in year after year, and new discoveries call for correction and rearrangement of what has been previously taught. It is also well that they should know that by the time the newest theory reaches the school-room and textbook it may be already antiquated and perhaps superseded in the observatory and laboratory, so that in scientific matters the school-room must always be a little "behind the times." And likewise that when scientific teaching has to be brought within the compass of a text-book for young students, it is mere baby talk, as much like the original theory as a toy engine is like an express locomotive. From which they may conclude that it is wiser to be listeners or to ask deferential questions than to have light-hearted opinions of their own on burning questions such as we sometimes hear: "Do you believe in evolution?--I do." "No, I don't, I think there is very little evidence for it." And that if they are introduced to a man of science it is better not to ask his opinion about the latest skeleton that has been discovered, or let him see that they are alarmed lest there might be something wrong with our pedigree after all, or with the book of Genesis. One would be glad, however, that they should know the names and something of the works and reputation of the Catholic men of science, as Ampere, Pasteur, and Wassmann, etc., I Who have been or are European authorities in special aches of study, so that they may at least be ready with an answer to the frequent assertion that "Catholics have done nothing for science."

But in connexion with these three subjects, not as to the teaching of them but as to their place in the education of girls, some points regarding education in general are worth considering:--

1. Mathematics in the curriculum of girls' schools has been the subject of much debate. Cool and colourless as mathematics are in themselves, they have produced in discussion a good deal of heat, being put forward to bear the brunt of the controversy as to whether girls were equal to boys in understanding and capable of following the same course of study, and to enter into competition with them in all departments of learning. Even taking into consideration many brilliant achievements and an immense amount of creditable, and even distinguished work, the answer of those who have no personal bias in the matter for the sake of a Cause--is generally that they are not. Facts would seem to speak for themselves if only on the ground that the strain of equal studies is too great for the weaker physical organization. Girls are willing workers, exceedingly intense when their heart is set upon success; but their staying power is not equal to their eagerness, and the demands made upon them sometimes leave a mortgage on their mental and physical estate which cannot be paid off in the course of a whole lifetime. In support of this, reference may be made to the [1 Appendix to "Final Report of the Commissioners (Irish Intermediate Education)," Pt. I, 1899.] report of a commission of Dublin physicians on the effects of the Intermediate Education system in Ireland, which has broken down many more girls than boys.

Apart from the question of over-pressure it is generally recognized--let it be said again, by those who have not a position to defend or a theory to advance in the matter--that the aptitude of girls for mathematical work is generally less than that of boys, and unless one has some particular view or plan at stake in the matter there is no grievance in recognizing this. There is more to be gained in recognizing diversities of gifts than in striving to establish a level of uniformity, and life is richer, not poorer for the setting forth of varied types of excellence. Competition destroys cooperation, and in striving to prove ability to reach an equal standard in competition, the wider and more lasting interests which are at stake may be lost sight of, and in the end sacrificed to limited temporary success.

The success of girls in the field of mathematics is, in general, temporary and limited, it means much less in their after life than in that of boys. For the few whose calling in life is teaching, mathematics have some after use; for those, still fewer, who take a real interest in them, they keep a place in later life; but for the many into whose life-work they do not enter, beyond the mental discipline which is sometimes evaded, very little remains. The end of school means for them the end of mathematical study, and the Complete forgetfulness in which the whole subject is soon buried gives the impression that too much may have been sacrificed to it. From the point of view of practical value it proves of little use, and as mental discipline something of more permanent worth might have taken its place to strengthen the reasoning powers. The mathematical teacher of girls has generally to seek consolation in very rare success for much habitual disappointment.

The whole controversy about equality in education involves less bitterness to Catholics than to others, for this reason, that we have less difficulty than

those of other persuasions in accepting a
fundamental difference of ideals for girls and boys.
Our ideals of family life, of spheres of action which
co-operate and complete each other, without
interference or competition, our masculine and
feminine types of holiness amongst canonized
saints, give a calmer outlook upon the questions
involved in the discussion. The Church puts
equality and inequality upon such a different
footing that the result is harmony without clash of
interests, and if in some countries we are drawn into
the arena now, and forced into competition, the very
slackness of interest which is sometimes
complained of is an indirect testimony to the truth
that we know of better things. And as those who
know of better things are more injured by following
the less good than those who know them not, so our
Catholic girls seem to be either more indifferent
about their work or more damaged by the spirit of
competition if they enter into it, than those who
consider it from a different plane.

2. Natural science has of late years assumed a title
to which it has no claim, and calls itself simply
"_Science_"--presumably "_for short,_" but to the
great confusion of young minds, or rather with the
effect of contracting their range of vision within
very narrow limits, as if theology and Biblical
study, and mental and moral, and historical and
political science, had no place of mention in the
rational order where things are studied in their
causes.

Inquiry was made in several schools where natural
science was taught according to the syllabuses of

the Board of Education. The question was asked, "What is science?"--and without exception the answers indicated that science was understood to mean the study of the phenomena of the physical world in their causes. The name "Science" used by itself has been the cause of this, and has led to the usual consequences of the assumption of unauthorized titles.

Things had been working up in England during the last few years towards this misconception in the schools. On the one hand there was the great impetus given to physical research and experimental science in recent years, so that its discoveries absorbed more and more attention, and this filtered down to the school books.

On the other hand, especially since the South African war, there had been a great stir in reaction against mere lessons from books, and it was seen that we wanted more personal initiative and thought, and resourcefulness, and self-reliance, and many other qualities which our education had not tended to develop. It was seen that we were unpractical in our Instruction, that minds passed under the discipline of school and came out again, still slovenly, unobservant, unscientific in temper, impatient, flippant, inaccurate, tending to guess and to jump at conclusions, to generalize hastily, etc. It was observed that many unskilful hands came out of the schools, clumsy ringers, wanting in neatness, untidy in work, inept in measuring and weighing, incapable of handling things intelligently. There had come an awakening from the dreams of 1870, when we felt so certain that all England was to be made good and happy through books. A remedy was sought in natural science, and the next educational wave which was to roll over us began to rise. It was thought that the temper of the really scientific man, so patient in research, so accurate and conscientious, so slow to dogmatize, so deferential to others, might be fostered by experimental science in the schools, acquiring "knowledge at first hand," making experiments, looking with great respect at balances, weighing and measuring, and giving an account of results. So laboratories were fitted up at great expense, and teachers with university degrees in science were sought after. The height of the tide seemed to be reached in 1904 and 1905--to judge by the tone of Regulations for the Curricula of Secondary Schools issued by the Board of Education--for in these years it is most insistent and exacting for girls as well as boys, as to time and scope of the syllabus in this branch. Then disillusion seems to have set in and the tide began to ebb. It appeared that the results were small and poor in proportion to expectation and to the outlay on laboratories. The desirable qualities did not seem to develop as had been hoped, the temper of mind fostered was not entirely what had been desired. The conscientious accuracy that was to come of measuring a millimetre and weighing a milligramme was disappointing, and also the fluent readiness to give an account of observations made, the desired accuracy of expression, the caution in drawing inferences. The links between this teaching and after life did not seem to be satisfactorily established. The Board of Education showed the first signs of a change of outlook by the readjustment in the curriculum giving an alternative syllabus for girls, and the latitude in this direction is widening by degrees. It begins to be whispered that even in some boys' schools the laboratory is only used under compulsion or by exceptional students, and the wave seems likely to go down as rapidly as it rose.

Probably for girls the strongest argument against experimental science taught in laboratories is that it has so little connexion with after life. As a discipline the remedy did not go deeply enough into the realities of life to reach the mental defects of girls; it was artificial, and they laid it aside as a part of school life when they went home. Latitude is now given by the Board of Education for "an approved course in a combination of the following subjects: needlework, cooking, laundry-work, housekeeping, and household hygiene for girls over fifteen years of age, to be substituted partially or wholly for science and for mathematics other than arithmetic." Comparing this with the regulations of five or six years ago when the only alternative for girls was a "biological subject" instead of physics, and elementary hygiene as a substitute for chemistry, it would seem as if the Board of Education had had reason to be dissatisfied with the "science" teaching for girls, and was determined to seek a more practical system.

This practical aspect of things is penetrating into every department, and when it is combined with some study of first principles nothing better can be desired. For instance, in the teaching of geography, of botany, etc., there is a growing inclination to follow the line of reality, the middle course between the book alone and the laboratory alone, so that these subjects gather living interest from their many points of contact with human life, and give more play to the powers of children. As the text-book of geography is more and more superseded by the use of the atlas alone, and the botanical chart by the children's own drawings, and by the beautiful illustrations in books prepared especially for them, the way is opened before them to worlds of beauty and wonder which they may have for their own possession by the use of their eyes and ears and thoughts and reasonings.

3. But better than all new apparatus and books of delight is the informal study of the world around us which has grown up by the side of organized teaching of natural science. The name of "nature study" is the least attractive point about it; the reality escapes from all conventionalities of instruction, and looks and listens and learns without the rules and boundaries which belong to real lessons. Its range is not restricted within formal limits; it is neither botany, nor natural history, nor physics; neither instruction on light nor heat nor sound, but it wanders on a voyage of discovery into all these domains. And in so far as it does this, it appeals very strongly to children. Children usually delight in flowers and dislike botany, are fond of animals and rather indifferent to natural history. Life is what awakens their interest; they love the living thing as a whole and do not care much for analysis or classification; these interests grow up later.

The object of informal nature study is to put

children directly in touch with the beautiful and wonderful things which are within their reach. Its lesson-book is everywhere, its time is every time, its spirit is wonder and delight. This is for the children. Those who teach it have to look beyond, and it is not so easy to teach as it is to learn. It cannot, properly speaking, be learned by teachers out of books, though books can do a great deal. But a long-used quiet habit of observation gives it life and the stored-up sweetness of years--"the old is better." The most charming books on nature study necessarily give a second-hand tone to the teaching. But the point of it all is knowledge at first-hand; yet, for children knowledge at first-hand is so limited that some one to refer to, and some one to guide them is a necessity, some one who will say at the right moment "look" and "listen," and who has looked and listened for years. Perhaps the requirement of knowledge at firsthand for children has sometimes been pushed a little too far, with a deadening effect, for the progress of such knowledge is very slow and laborious. How little we should know if we only admitted first-hand knowledge, but the stories of wonder from those who have seen urge us on to see for ourselves; and so we swing backwards and forwards, from the world outside to the books, to find out more, from the books to the world outside to see for ourselves. And a good teacher, who is an evergreen learner, goes backwards and forwards, too, sharing the work and heightening the delight. All the stages come in turn, over and over again, observation, experiment, inquiry from others whether orally or in books, and in this subject books abound more fascinating than fairy tales, and their latest charm is that they are laying aside the pose of a fairy tale and tell the simple truth.

The love of nature, awakened early, is a great estate with which to endow a child, but it needs education, that the proprietor of the estate may know how to manage it, and not--with the manners of a _parvenu_--miss either the inner spirit or the outward behaviour belonging to the property. This right manner and spirit of possession is what the informal "nature study" aims at; it is a point of view. Now the point of view as to the outside world means a great deal in life. Countrymen do not love nature as townsmen love it. Their affection is deeper but less emotional, like old friendships, undemonstrative but everlasting. Countrymen see without looking, and say very little about it. Townsmen in the country look long and say what they have seen, but they miss many things. A farmer stands stolidly among the graces of his frisky lambs and seems to miss their meaning, but this is because the manners cultivated in his calling do not allow the expression of feeling. It is all in his soul somewhere, deeply at home, but impossible to utter. The townsman looks eagerly, expresses a great deal, expresses it well, but misses the spirit from want of a background to his picture. One must know the whole round of the year in the country to catch the spirit of any season and perceive whence it comes and whither it goes.

On the other hand, the countryman in town thinks that there is no beauty of the world left for him to see, because the spirit there is a spirit of the hour and not of the season, and natural beauty has to be caught in evanescent appearances--a florist's window full of orchids in place of his woodlands-- and his mind is too slow to catch these. This too quick or too slow habit of seeing belongs to minds as well as to callings; and when children are learning to look around them at the world outside, it has to be taken into account. Some will see without looking and be satisfied slowly to drink in impressions, and they are really glad to learn to express what they see. Others, the quick, so-called "clever" children, look, and judge, and comment, and overshoot the mark many times before they really see. These may learn patience in waiting for their garden seeds, and quietness from watching birds and beasts, and deliberation, to a certain extent, from their constant mistakes. To have the care of plants may teach them a good deal of watchfulness and patience; it is of greater value to a child to have grown one perfect flower than to have pulled many to pieces to examine their structure. And the care of animals may teach a great deal more if it learns to keep the balance between silly idolatry of pets and cruel negligence--the hot and cold extremes of selfishness.

Little gardens of their own are perhaps the best gifts which can be given to children. To work in them stores up not only health but joy. Every flower in their garden stands for so much happiness, and with that happiness an instinct for home life and simple pleasures will strike deep roots. From growing the humblest annual out of a seed-packet to grafting roses there is work for every age, and even in the dead season of the year the interest of a garden never dies.

In new countries gardens take new aspects. A literal version of a *garden party* in the Transvaal suggests possibilities of emancipation from the conventionalities which weary the older forms of entertainment with us. Its object was not to play in a garden, but to plant one. Guests came from afar, each one bringing a contribution of plants. The afternoon was spent in laying out the beds and planting the offerings, in hard, honest, dirty work. And all the guests went home feeling that they had really lived a day that was worth living, for a garden had been made, in the rough, it is true; but even in the rough in such a new country a garden is a great possession.

The outcome of these considerations is that the love of nature is a great source of happiness for children, happiness of the best kind in taking possession of a world that seems to be in many ways designed especially for them. It brings their minds to a place where many ways meet; to the confines of science, for they want to know the reasons of things; to the confines of art, for what they can understand they will strive to interpret and express; to the confines of worship, for a child's soul, hushed in wonder, is very near to God.

CHAPTER VIII.

ENGLISH.

"If Chaucer, as has been said, is Spring, it is a modern, premature Spring, followed by an interval of doubtful weather. Sidney is the very Spring--the later May. And in prose he is the authentic, only Spring. It is a prose full of young joy, and young power, and young inexperience, and young melancholy, which is the wilfulness of joy; . . .

"Sidney's prose is treasureable, not only for its absolute merits, but as the bud from which English prose, that gorgeous and varied flower, has unfolded."--FRANCIS THOMPSON, "The Prose of Poets."

The study of one's own language is the very heart of a modern education; to the study of English, therefore, belongs a central place in the education of English-speaking girls. It has two functions: one is to become the instrument by which almost all the other subjects are apprehended; the other, more characteristically its own, is to give that particular tone to the mind which distinguishes it from others. This is a function that is always in process of further development; for the mind of a nation elaborates its language, and the language gives tone to the mind of the new generation. The influences at work upon the English language at present are very complex, and play on it with great force, so that the changes are startling in their rapidity. English is not only the language of a nation or of a race, not even of an empire; and the inflowing elements affirm this. We have kindred beyond the empire, and their speech is more and more impressing ours, forging from the common stock, which they had from us, whole armouries full of expressive words, words with edge and point and keen directness which never miss the mark. Some are unquestionably an acquisition, those which come from States where the language is honoured and studied with a carefulness that puts to shame all except our very best. They have kept some gracious and rare expressions, now quaint to our ear, preserved out of Elizabethan English in the current speech of to-day. These have a fragrance of the olden time, but we cannot absorb them again into our own spoken language. Then they have their incisive modern expressions so perfectly adapted for their end that they are irresistible even to those who cling by tradition to the more stable element in English. These also come from States in which language is conscious of itself and looks carefully to literary use, and they do us good rather than harm. Other importations from younger States are too evidently unauthorized to be in any way beautiful, and are blamed on both sides of the ocean as debasing the coinage. But these, too, are making their way, so cheap and convenient are they, and so expressive.

It is needful in educating children to remember that this strong inflowing current must be taken into account, and also to remember that it does not belong to them. They must first be trained in the use of the more lasting elements of English; later on they may use their discretion in catching the new words which are afloat in the air, but the foundations must be laid otherwise. It takes the bloom off the freshness of young writers if they are determined to exhibit the last new words that are in, or out of season. New words have a doubtful position at first. They float here and there like thistle-down, and their future depends upon where they settle. But until they are established and accepted they are out of place for children's use. They are contrary to the perfect manner for children. We ask that their English should be simple and unaffected, not that it should glitter with the newest importations, brilliant as they may be. It is from the more permanent element in the language that they will acquire what they ought to have, the characteristic traits of thought and manner which belong to it. It is not too much to look for such things in children's writing and speaking. The first shoots and leaves may come up early though the full growth and flower may be long waited for. These characteristics are often better put into words by foreign critics than by ourselves, for we are inclined to take them as a whole and to take them for granted; hence the trouble experienced by educated foreigners in catching the characteristics of English style, and their surprise in finding that we have no authentic guides to English composition, fend that the court of final appeal is only the standard Of the best use. The words of a German critic on a Collection of English portraits in Berlin are very happily pointed and might be as aptly applied to writing as to painting.

"English, utterly English! Nothing on God's earth could be more English than this whole collection. The personality of the artist (_it happened that he was an Irishman_), the countenances of the subjects, their dress, the discreetly suggestive backgrounds, all have the characteristic touch of British culture, very refined, very high-bred, very quiet, very much clarified, very confident, very neat, very well-appointed, a little dreamy and just a little wearisome--the precise qualities which at the same time impress and annoy us in the English."

This is exactly what might be said of Pater's writing, but that is full-grown English. Pater is not a model for children, they would find him more than "just a little wearisome." If anyone could put into words what Sir Joshua Reynolds' portraits of children express, that would be exactly what we want for the model of their English. They can write and they can speak in a beautiful way of their own if they are allowed a little liberty to grow wild, and trained a little to climb. Their charm is candour, as it is the charm of Sir Joshua's portraits, with a quiet confidence that all is well in the world they know, and that everyone is kind; this gives the look of trustful innocence and unconcern. Their writing and talking have this charm, as long as nothing has happened to make them conscious of themselves. But these first blossoms drop off, and there is generally an intermediate stage in which they can neither speak nor write, but keep their thoughts close, and will not give themselves away. Only when that stage is past do they really and with full consciousness seek to express themselves, and pay some attention to the self-expression of others. This third stage has its May-day, when the things which have become hackneyed to our minds from long use come to them with the full force of revelations, and they astonish us by their exuberant delight. But they have a right to their May-day and it ought not to be cut short; the sun will go down of itself, and then June will come in its own time and ripen the green wood, and after that will come pruning time, in another season, and then the phase of severity and fastidiousness, and after that--if they continue to write--they will be truly themselves.

In every stage we have our duty to do, encouraging and pruning by turns, and, as in everything else, we must begin with ourselves and go on with ourselves that there may be always something living to give, and some growth; for in this we need never cease to grow, in knowledge, in taste, and in critical power. The means are not far to seek; if we really care about these things, the means are everywhere, in reading the best things, in taking notes, in criticising independently and comparing with the best criticism, in forming our own views and yet keeping a willingness to modify them, in an attitude of mind that is always learning, always striving, always raising its standard, never impatient but permanently dissatisfied.

We have three spheres of action in the use of the language--there is English to speak, English to write, And the wide field of English to read, and there are vital interests bound up in each for the after life of children. As they speak, so will be the tone of their intercourse; as they write, so will be the standard of their habits of thought; and as they read so will be the atmosphere of their life, and the preparation of their judgment for those critical moments of choice which are the pivots upon which its whole action moves.

If practice alone would develop it to perfection, speaking ought to be easy to learn, but it does not prove so, and especially when children are together in schools the weeds grow faster than the crop, and the crop is apt to be thin. The language of the majority holds its own; children among children can express with a very small vocabulary what they want to say to each other, whereas an only child who lives with its elders has usually a larger vocabulary than it can manage, which makes the sayings of only children quaint and almost weird, as the perfection of the instrument persuades us that there is a full-grown thought within it, and a child's fancy suddenly laughs at us from under the disguise.

There is general lamentation at present because the art of conversation has fallen to a very low ebb; there is, in particular, much complaint of the conversation of girls whose education is supposed to have been careful. The subjects they care to talk of are found to be few and poor, their power of expressing themselves very imperfect, the scanty words at their command worked to death in supplying for all kinds of things to which they are not appropriate. We know that we have a great deal of minted gold in the English language, but little of it finds its way into our general conversation, most of our intercourse is carried on with small change, a good deal of it even in coppers, and the worst trouble of all is that so few seem to care or to regret it. Perhaps the young generation will do so later in life, but unless something is done for them during the years of their education it does not seem probable, except in the case of the few who are driven by their professional work to think of it, or drawn to it by some influence that compels them to exert themselves in earnest.

Listening to the conversation of girls whose thoughts and language are still in a fluid state, say from the age of 17 to 25, gives a great deal of matter for thought to those who are interested in education, and this point of language is of particular interest. There are the new catch-words of each year; they had probably a great *piquancy* in the mouth of the originator but they very soon become flat by repetition, then they grow jaded, are more and more neglected and pass away altogether. From their rising to their setting the arc is very short-- about five years seems to be the limit of their existence, and no one regrets them. We do not seem to be in a happy vein of development at present as to the use of words, and these short-lived catch-words are generally poor in quality. Our girl talkers are neither rich nor independent in their language, they lay themselves under obligations to anyone who will furnish a new catch-word, and especially to boys from whom they take rather than accept contributions of a different kind. It is an old-fashioned regret that girls should copy boys instead of developing themselves independently in language and manners; but though old-fashioned, it will never cease to be true that what was made to be beautiful on its own line is dwarfed and crippled by straining it into imitation of something else which it can never be.

What can be done for the girls to give them first more independence in their language and then more power to express themselves? Probably the best cure, food and tonic in one, is reading; a taste for the best reading alters the whole condition of mental life, and without being directly attacked the defects in conversation will correct themselves. But we could do more than is often done for the younger children, not by talking directly about these things, but by being a little harder to please, and giving when it is possible the cordial commendation which makes them feel that what they have done was worth working for.

Recitation and reading aloud, besides all their other uses, have this use that they accustom children to the sound of their own voices uttering beautiful words, which takes away the odd shyness which some of them feel in going beyond their usual round of expressions and extending their vocabulary. We owe it to our language as well as to each individual child to make recitation and reading aloud as beautiful as possible. Perhaps one of the causes of our conversational slovenliness is the neglect of these; critics of an older generation have not ceased to lament their decay, but it seems as if better times were coming again, and that as the fundamentals of breathing and voice-production are taught, we shall increase the scope of the power acquired and give it more importance. There is a great deal underlying all this, beyond the acquirement of voice and pronunciation. If recitation is cultivated there is an inducement to learn by heart; this in its turn ministers to the love of reading and to the formation of literary taste, and enriches the whole life of the mind. There is an indirect but far-reaching gain of self-possession, from the need for outward composure and inward concentration of mind in reciting before others. But it is a matter of importance to choose recitations so that nothing should be learnt which must be thrown away, nothing which is not worth remembering for life. It is a pity to make children acquire what they will soon despise when they might learn something that they will grow up to and prize as long as they live. There are beautiful things that they can understand, if something is wanted for to-day, which have at the same time a life that will never be outgrown. There are poems with two aspects, one of which is acceptable to a child and the other to the grown-up mind; these, one is glad to find in anthologies for children. But there are many poems about children of which the interest is so subtle as to be quite unsuitable for their collection. Such a poem is "We are seven." Children can be taught to say it, even with feeling, but their own genuine impression of it seems to be that the little girl was rather weak in intellect for eight years old, or a little perverse. Whereas Browning's "An incident of the French camp" appeals to them by pride of courage as it does to us by pathos. It may not be a gem, poetically speaking, but it lives. As children grow older it is only fair to allow them some choice in what they learn and recite, to give room for their taste to follow its own bent; there are a few things which it is well that every one should know by heart, but beyond these the field is practically without limits.

Perfect recitation or reading aloud is very rare and difficult to acquire. For a few years there was a tendency to over-emphasis in both, and, in recitation, to teach gesture, for which as a nation we are singularly inapt. This is happily disappearing, simplicity and restraint are regaining their own, at least in the best teaching for girls. As to reading aloud to children it begins to be recognized that it should not be too explicit, nor too emphatic, nor too pointed; that it must leave something for the natural grace of the listener's intelligence to supply and to feel. There is a didactic tone in reading which says, "you are most unintelligent, but listen to ME and there may yet be hope that you will understand." This leaves the "poor creatures" of the class still unmoved and unenlightened; "the child is not awakened," while the more sensitive minds are irritated; they can feel it as an impertinence without quite knowing why they are hurt. It is a question of manners and consideration which is perceptible to them, for they like what is best--sympathy and suggestiveness rather than hammering in. They can help each other by their simple insight into these things when they read aloud, and if a reading lesson in class is conducted as an exercise in criticism it is full of interest. The frank good-nature and gravity of twelve-year-old critics makes their operations quite painless, and they are accepted with equal good humour and gravity, no one wasting any emotion and a great deal of good sense being exchanged.

Conversation, as conversation, is hard to teach, we can only lead the way and lay down a few principles which keep it in the right path. These commonplaces of warning, as old as civilization itself, belong to manners and to fundamental unselfishness, but obvious as they are they have to be said and to be repeated and enforced until they become matters of course. Not to seem bored, not to interrupt, not to contradict, not to make personal remarks, not to talk of oneself (some one was naive enough to say "then what is there to talk of"), not to get heated and not to look cold, not to do all the talking and not to be silent, not to advance if the ground seems uncertain, and to be sensitively attentive to what jars--all these and other things are troublesome to obtain, but exceedingly necessary. And even observing them all we may be just as far from conversation as before; how often among English people, through shyness or otherwise, it simply faints from inanition. We can at least teach that a first essential is to have something to say, and that the best preparation of mind is thought and reading and observation, to be interested in many things, and to give enough personal application to a few things as to have something worth saying about them.

By testing in writing every step of an educational course a great deal of command over all acquired materials may be secured. As our girls grow older, essay-writing becomes the most powerful means for fashioning their minds and bringing out their individual characteristics.

It is customary now to begin with oral composition,--quite rightly, for one difficulty at a time is enough. But when children have to write for themselves the most natural beginning is by letters. A great difference in thought and power is observable in their first attempts, but in the main the structure of their letters is similar, like the houses and the moonfaced persons which they draw in the

same symbolic way. Perhaps both are accepted
conventions to which they conform--handed down
through generations of the nursery tradition--though
students of children are inclined to believe that
these symbolical drawings represent their real mind
in the representation of material things. Their
communications move in little bounds, a succession
of happy thoughts, the kind of things which birds in
conversation might impart to one another, turning
their heads quickly from side to side and catching
sight of many things unrelated amongst themselves.
It is a pity that this manner is often allowed to last
too long, for in these stages of mental training it is
better to be on the stretch to reach the full stature of
one's age rather than to linger behind it, and early
promise in composition means a great deal.

To write of the things which belong to one's age in
a manner that is fully up to their worth or even a
little beyond it, is better than to strain after
something to say in a subject that is beyond the
mental grasp. The first thing to learn is how to write
pleasantly about the most simple and ordinary
things. But a common fault in children's writing is
to wait for an event, "something to write about,"
and to dispose of it in three or four sentences like
telegrams.

The influences which determine these early steps
are, first, the natural habit of mind, for thoughtful
children see most interesting and strange things in
their surroundings; secondly, the tone of their
ordinary conversation, but especially a disposition
that is unselfish and affectionate. Warm-hearted
children who are gifted with sympathy have an

intuition of what will give pleasure, and that is one of the great secrets of letter-writing. But the letters they write will always depend in a great measure on the letters they receive, and a family gift for letter-writing is generally the outcome of a happy home-life in which all the members are of interest to each other and their doings of importance.

What sympathy gives to letter-writing, imagination gives to the first essays of children in longer compositions. Imagination puts them in sympathy with all the world, with things as well as persons, as affection keeps them in touch with every detail of the home world. But its work is not so simple. Home affection is true and is a law to itself; if it is present it holds all the little child's world in a right proportion, because all heavenly affection is bound up with it. But the awakening and the rapid development of imagination as girls grow up needs a great deal of guidance and training. Fancy may overgrow itself, and take an undue predominance, so that life is tuned to the pitch of imagination and not imagination to the pitch of life. It is hardly possible and hardly to be desired that it should never overflow the limits of perfect moderation; if it is to be controlled, there must be something to control, in pruning there must be some strong shoots to cut back, and in toning down there must be some over-gaudy colours to subdue. It is better that there should be too much life than too little, and better that criticism should find something vigorous enough to lay hold of, rather than something which cannot be felt at all. This is the time to teach children to begin their essays without preamble, by something that they really want to say, and to finish them leaving something still unsaid that they would like to have expressed, so as not to pour out to the last drop their mind or their fancy on any subject. This discipline of promptitude in beginning and restraint at the end will tell for good upon the quality of their writing.

But the work of the imagination may also betray something unreal and morbid--this is a more serious fault and means trouble coming. It generally points to a want of focus in the mind; because self predominates in the affections feeling and interest are self-centred. Then the whole development of mind comes to a disappointing check--the mental power remains on the level of unstable sixteen years old, and the selfish side develops either emotionally or frivolously--according to taste, faster than it can be controlled.

There are cross-roads at about sixteen in a girl's life. After two or three troublesome years she is going to make her choice, not always consciously and deliberately, but those who are alive to what is going on may expect to hear about this time her speech from the throne, announcing what the direction of her life is going to be. It is not necessarily the choice of a vocation in life, that belongs to an order of things that has neither day nor hour determined for it, but it is when the mental outlook takes a direction of its own, literary, or artistic, or philosophical, or worldly, or turning towards home; it may sometimes be the moment of decisive vocation to leave all things for God, or, as has so often happened in the lives of the Saints, the time when a child's first desire, forgotten for a while, asserts itself again. In any case it is generally a period of new awakenings, and if things are as they ought to be, generally a time of deep happiness--the ideal hour in the day of our early youth. All this is faithfully rendered in the essays of that time; we unsuspectingly give ourselves away.

After this, for those who are going to write at all, comes the "viewy" stage, and this is full of interest. We are so dogmatic, so defiant, so secure in our persuasions. It is impossible to believe that they will ever alter. Yet who has lived through this phase of abounding activity and has not found that, at first with the shock of disappointment, and afterwards without regret, a memorial cross had to be set by our wayside, here and there, marking the place of rest for our most enthusiastic convictions. In the end one comes to be glad of it, for if it means anything it means a growth in the truth.

The criticism of essays is one of the choice opportunities which education offers, for then the contact of mind with mind is so close that truth can be told under form of criticism, which as exhortation would have been less easily accepted. It is evident that increasing freedom must be allowed as the years go on, and that girls have a right to their own taste and manner--and within the limits of their knowledge to form their own opinions; but it is in this period of their development that they are most sensitive to the mental influence of those who are training them, and their quick responsiveness to the best is a constant stimulus to go on for their sakes, discovering and tasting and training one's discernment in what is most excellent.

From this point we may pass to what is first in the
order of things--but first and last in this department
of an English education--and that is reading, with
the great field of literature before us, and the duty of
making the precious inheritance all that it ought to
be to this young generation of ours--heiresses to all
its best.

English literature will be to children as they grow
up, what we have made it to them in the beginning.
There will always be the exceptional few,
privileged ones, who seem to have received the key
to it as a personal gift. They will find their way
without us, but if we have the honour of rendering
them service we may do a great deal even for them
in showing where the best things lie, and the way to
make them one's own. But the greater number have
to be taken through the first steps with much
thought and discernment, for taste in literature is
not always easy to develop, and may be spoiled by
bad management at the beginning. We are not very
teachable as a nation in this matter--our young taste
is wayward, and sometimes contradictory, it will
not give account of itself, very likely it cannot. We
have inarticulate convictions that this is right, and
suits us, and something else is wrong as far as our
taste is concerned, and that we have rights to like
what we like and condemn what we do not like, and
we have gone a considerable way along the road
before we can stop and look about us and see the
reason of our choice. English literature itself fosters
this independent spirit of criticism by its
extraordinary abundance, its own wide liberty of
spirit, its surpassing truthfulness. Our greatest poets
and our truest do not sing to an audience but to their

Maker and to His world, and let anyone who can understand it catch the song, and sing it after them. No doubt many have fallen from the truth and piped an artificial tune, and they have had their following. But love for the real and true is very deep and in the end it prevails, and as far as we can obtain it with children it must prevail.

Their first acquaintance with beautiful things is best established by reading aloud to them, and this need not be limited entirely to what they can understand at the time. Even if we read something that is beyond them, they have listened to the cadences, they have heard the song without the words, the words will come to them later. If there is good ground for the seed to fall upon, and we sow good seed, it will come up with its thirtyfold or more, as seed sown in the mind seems always to come up, whether it be good or bad, and even if it has lain dormant for years. There are good moments laid up in store for the future when the words, which have been familiar for years, suddenly awake to life, and their meaning, full-grown, at the moment when we need it, or at the moment when we are able to understand its value, dawns upon the mind. Then we are grateful to those who invested these revenues for us though we knew it not. We are not grateful to those who give us the less good though pleasant and easy to enjoy. A little severity and fastidiousness render us better service. And this is especially true for girls, since for them it is above all important that there should be a touch of the severe in their taste, and that they should be a little exacting, for if they once let themselves go to what is too light-heartedly popular they do not know where to draw the line and they go very far, with great loss to themselves and others.

One of the beautiful things of to-day in England is the wealth of children's literature. It is a peculiar grace of our time that we are all trying to give the best to the children, and this is most of all remarkable in the books published for them. We had rather a silly moment in which we kept them babies too long and thought that rhymes without reason would please them, and another moment when we were just a little morbid about them; but now we have struck a very happy vein, free from all morbidness, very innocent and very happy, abounding in life and in no way unfitting for the experiences that have to be lived through afterwards. No one thinks it waste of time to write and illustrate books for children, and to do their very best in both, and the result of historical research and the most critical care of texts is put within the children's reach with a real understanding of what they can care for. A true appreciation of the English classics must result from this, and the mere reading of what is choice is an early safeguard against the less good.

Reading, without commentary, is what is best accepted; we are beginning to come back to this belief. It is agreed almost generally that there has been too much comment and especially too much analysis in our teaching of literature, and that the majesty or the loveliness of our great writers' works have not been allowed to speak for themselves. We have not trusted them enough, and we have not trusted the children so much as they deserved. The little boy who said he could understand if only they would not explain has become historical, and his word of warning, though it may not have sounded quite respectful, has been taken into account. We have now fewer of the literary Baedeker's guides who stopped us at particular points, to look back for the view, and gave the history and date of the work with its surrounding circumstances, and the meaning of every word, while they took away the soul of the poem, and robbed us of our whole impression. We realize now that by reading and reading again, until they have mastered the music, and the meaning dawns of itself, children gain more than the best annotations can give them; these will be wanted later on, but in the beginning they set the attitude of mind completely wrong for early literary study in which reverence and receptiveness and delight are of more account than criticism. The memory of these things is so much to us in after life, and if the living forms of beautiful poems have been torn to pieces to show us the structure within, and the matter has been shaken out into ungainly paraphrase and pursued with relentless analysis until it has given up the last secret of its meaning, the remembrance of this destructive process will remain and the spirit will never be the same again. The best hope for beautiful memories is in perfect reading aloud, with that reverence of mind and reticence of feeling which keeps itself in the background, not imposing a marked per-Bonal interpretation, but holding up the poem with enough support to make it speak for itself and no more. There is a vexed question about the reading allowed to girls which cannot be entirely passed over. It is a point on which authorities differ widely among themselves, according to the standard of their family, the whole early training which has given their mind a particular bent, the quality of their own taste and their degree of sensitiveness and insight, the views which they hold about the character of girls, their ideas of the world and the probable future surroundings of those whom they advise, as well as many other considerations. It is quite impossible to arrive at a uniform standard, or at particular precepts or at lists of books or authors which should or should not be allowed. Even if these could be drawn up, it would be more and more difficult to enforce them or to keep the rules abreast of the requirements of each publishing season. In reading, as in conduct, each one must bear more and more of their own personal responsibility, and unless the law is within themselves there is no possibility of enforcing it.

The present Cardinal Archbishop of Westminster, when rector of St. John's Seminary, Wonersh, used to lay down the following rules for his students, and on condition of their adhering to these rules he allowed them great freedom in their reading, but if they were disregarded, it was understood that the rector took no responsibility about the books they read:--

1. "Be perfectly conscientious, and if you find a book is doing you harm stop reading it at once. If you know you cannot stop you must be most careful not to read anything you don't know about."

2. "Be perfectly frank with your confessor and other superiors. Don't keep anything hidden from them."

3. "Don't recommend books to others which,
although they may do no harm to you, might do
harm to them."

These rules are very short but they call for a great
deal of self-control, frankness, and discretion. They
set up an inward standard for the conscience, and, if
honestly followed, they answer in practice any
difficulty that is likely to arise as to choice of
reading. [1--In the Appendix will be found a
pastoral letter by Cardinal Bourne, Archbishop of
Westminster, then Bishop of Southwark, bearing on
this subject and full of instruction for all who have
to deal with it.]

But the application of these rules presupposes a
degree of judgment and self-restraint which are
hardly to be found in girls of school-room years,
and before they can adjust themselves to the relative
standard and use the curb for themselves, it is
necessary to set before them some fixed rules by
which to judge. While life is young and character
plastic and personal valuations still in formation,
the difficulty is to know what is harmful. "How am
I to know," such a one may ask, "whether what
seems harmful to me may not be really a gain,
giving me a richer life, a greater expansion of spirit,
a more independent and human character? May not
this effect which I take to be harm, be no more than
necessary growing pains; may it not be bringing me
into truer relation with life as it is, and as a whole?"

There will always be on one side timid and
mediocre minds, satisfied to shut themselves up and
safeguard what they already have; and on the other

more daring and able spirits who are tempted beyond the line of safety in a thirst for discovery and adventure, and are thus swept out beyond their own immature control. Books that foster the spirit of rebellion, of doubt and discontent concerning the essentials and inevitable elements of human life, that tend to sap the sense of personal responsibility, and to disparage the cardinal virtues and the duty of self-restraint as against impulse, are emphatically bad. They are particularly bad for girls with their impressionable minds and tendency to imitation, and inclination to be led on by the glamour of the old temptation; "Your eyes shall be opened; you shall be as gods, knowing good and evil."

To follow a doubt or a lie or a by-way of conduct with the curiosity to see what comes of it in the end, is to prepare their own minds for similar lines of thought and action, and in the crises of life, when they have to choose for themselves, often unadvised and without time to deliberate, they are more likely to fall by the doubt or the lie or the spirit of revolt which has become familiar to them in thought and sympathy.

CHAPTER IX.

MODERN LANGUAGES.

"All nations have their message from on high, Each the messiah of some central thought, For the fulfilment and delight of Man: One has to teach that Labour is divine; Another Freedom and another Mind; And all, that God is open-eyed and just, The happy centre and calm heart of all." JAMES RUSSELL LOWELL.

We cannot have a perfect knowledge even of our own language without some acquaintance with more than one other, either classical or modern. This is especially true of English because it has drawn its strength and wealth from so many sources, and absorbed them into itself. But this value is usually taken indirectly, by the way, and the understanding of it only comes to us after years as an appreciable good. It is, however, recognized that no education corresponding to the needs of our own time can be perfected or even adequately completed in one language alone. Not only do the actual conditions of life make it imperative to have more than one tongue at our command from the rapid extension of facilities for travelling, and increased intercourse with other nations; but in proportion to the cooling down of our extreme ardour for experimental science in the school-room we are returning to recognize in language a means of education more adapted to prepare children for life, by fitting them for intercourse with their fellow-creatures and giving them some appreciative understanding of the works of man's mind. Thus languages, and especially modern languages, are assuming more and more importance in the education of children, not only with us, but in most other countries of Europe. In some of them the methods are distinctly in advance of ours.

Much has been written of late years in the course of educational discussions as to the value of classical studies in education. As the best authorities are not yet in agreement among themselves it would be obviously out of place to add anything here on the subject. But the controversy principally belongs to classics in boys' schools; as to the study of Latin by girls, and in particular to its position in Catholic schools, there is perhaps something yet to be said.

In non-Catholic schools for girls Latin has not, even now, a great hold. It is studied for certain examinations, but except for the few students whose life takes a professional turn it scarcely outlives the school-room. Girl students at universities cannot compete on equal terms with men in a classical course, and the fact is very generally acknowledged by their choosing another. Except in the rarest instances--let us not be afraid to own it--our Latin is that of amateurs, brilliant amateurs perhaps, but unmistakable. Latin, for girls, is a source of delight, a beautiful enrichment of their mental life, most precious in itself and in its influence, but it is not a living power, nor a familiar instrument, nor a great discipline; it is deficient in hardness and closeness of grain, so that it cannot take polish; it is apt to betray by unexpected transgressions the want of that long, detailed, severe training which alone can make classical scholarship. It is usually a little

tremulous, not quite sure of itself, and indeed its
best adornment is generally the sobriety induced by
an overshadowing sense of paternal correction and
solicitude always present to check rashness and
desultoriness, and make it at least "gang warily"
with a finger on its lip; and their attainments in
Latin are, at the best, receptively rather than
actively of value.

In Catholic girls' schools, however, the elements of
Latin are almost necessity. It is wanting in courtesy,
it is almost uncouth for us to grow up without any
knowledge of the language of Holy Church. It is
almost impossible for educated Catholics to have
right taste in devotion, the "love and relish" of the
most excellent things, without some knowledge of
our great liturgical prayers and hymns in the
original. We never can really know them if we only
hear them halting and plunging and splashing
through translations, wasting their strength in many
words as they must unavoidably do in English, and
at best only reaching an approximation to the sense.
The use of them in the original is discipline and
devotion in one, and it strengthens the Catholic
historical hold on the past, with a sense of nearness,
when we dwell with some understanding on the
very words which have been sung in the Church
subsisting in all ages and teaching all nations. This
is our birthright, but it is not truly ours unless we
can in some degree make use of what we own.

It has often been pointed out that even to the most
uneducated amongst our people Latin is never a
dead language to Catholics, and that the familiar
prayers at Mass and public devotions make them at

home in the furthest countries of the earth as soon
as they are within the church doors. So far as this, it
is a universal language for us, and even if it went no
further than the world-wide home feeling of the
poor in our churches it would make us grateful for
every word of Latin that has a familiar sound to
them, and this alone might make us anxious to teach
Catholic children at school, for the use of prayer
and devotion, as much Latin as they can learn even
if they never touch a classic.

Our attitude towards the study of modern languages
has had its high and low tides within the last
century. We have had our submissive and our
obstinate moods; at present we are rather well and
affably disposed. French used to be acknowledged
without a rival as the universal language; it was a
necessity, and in general the older generation
learned it carefully and spoke it well. At that time
Italian was learned from taste and German was
exceptional. Queen Victoria's German marriage and
all the close connexion that followed from it
pressed the study of German to the front; the
influence of Carlyle told in the same direction, and
the study of Italian declined. Then in our
enthusiasm for physical sciences for a time we read
more German, but not German of the best quality,
and in another line we were influenced by German
literary criticism. Now, the balance of things has
altered again. For scholarship and criticism German
is in great request; in commercial education it is
being outrun by Spanish; for the intercourse of
ordinary life Germans are learning English much
more eagerly than we are learning German. We
have had a fit of--let us call it--shyness, but we are

trying to do better. We recognize that these fits of shyness are not altogether to our credit, not wholly reasonable, and that we are not incapable of learning foreign languages well. We know the story of the little boy reprimanded by the magistrate for his folly in running away from home because he was obliged to learn French, and his haughty reply that if foreigners wished to speak to him they might learn his language. But our children have outgrown him, as to his declaration if not as to his want of diligence, and we are in general reforming our methods of teaching so much that it will soon be inexcusable not to speak one or two languages well, besides our own.

The question of pronunciation and accent has been haunted by curious prejudices. An English accent in a foreign tongue has been for some speakers a refuge for their shyness, and for others a stronghold of their patriotism. The first of these feared that they would not be truly themselves unless their personality could take shelter beneath an accent that was unmistakably from England, and the others felt that it was like hauling down the British flag to renounce the long-drawn English "A-o-o." And, curiously, at the other extreme, the slightest tinge of an English accent is rather liked in Paris, perhaps only among those touched with Anglomania. But now we ought to be able to acquire whatever accent we choose, even when living far away from every instructor, having the gramophone to repeat to us untiringly the true Spanish "manana" and the French "ennui." And the study of phonetics, so much developed within the last few years, makes it unpardonable for teachers of modern languages to let the old English faults prevail.

We have had our succession of methods too. The old method of learning French, with a *bonne* in the nursery first, and then a severely academic governess or tutor, produced French of unsurpassed quality-But it belonged to home education, it required a great deal of leisure, it did not adapt itself to school curricula in which each child, to use the expressive American phrase, "carries" so many subjects that the hours and minutes for each have to be jealously counted out. There have been a series of methods succeeding one another which can scarcely be called more than quack methods of learning languages, claiming to be the natural method, the maternal method, the only rational method, etc. Educational advertisements of these have been magnificent in their promise, but opinions are not entirely at one as to the results.

The conclusions which suggest themselves after seeing several of these methods at work are:--

1. That good teachers can make use of almost any method with excellent results but that they generally evolve one of their own.

2. That if the teachers and the children take a great deal of trouble the progress will be very remarkable, whatever method is employed, and that without this both the classical and the "natural" methods can accomplish very little.

3. That teachers with fixed ideas about children and about methods arrest development.

4. That the self-instruction courses which "work out at a penny a lesson" (the lesson lasts ten minutes and is especially recommended for use in trams), and the gramophone with the most elaborate records, still bear witness to the old doctrine that there is no royal road to the learning of languages, and that it is not cheap in the end. In proportion to the value we set upon perfect acquirement of them will be our willingness to spend much labour upon foundations. By this road we arrive again at the fundamentals of an educator's calling, love and labour.

The value to the mind of acquiring languages is so great that all our trouble is repaid. It is not utilitarian value: what is merely for usefulness can be easily acquired, it has very little beauty. It is not for the sake of that commonplace usefulness that we should care to spend trouble upon permanent foundations in any tongue. The mind is satisfied only by the genius of the language, its choicest forms, its characteristic movement, and, most of all, the possession of its literature from within, that is to say of the spirit as it speaks to its own, and in which the language is most completely itself.

The special fitness of modern languages in a girl's education does not appear on the surface, and it requires more than a superficial, conversational knowledge to reap the fruit of their study. The social, and at present the commercial values are obvious to every one, and of these the commercial value is growing very loud in its assertions, and appears very exacting in its demands. For this the quack methods promise the short and easy way, and perhaps they are sufficient for it. A knowledge sufficient for business correspondence is not what belongs to a liberal education; it has a very limited range, hard, plain, brief communications, supported on cast-iron frames, inelastic forms and crudest courtesies, a mere formula for each particular case, and a small vocabulary suited to the dealings of every branch of business. We know the parallel forms of correspondence in English, which give a means of communication but not properly a language. Even the social values of languages are less than they used to be, as the finer art of conversation has declined. A little goes a long way; the rush of the motor has cut it short; there is not time to exchange more than a few commonplaces, and for these a very limited number of words is enough.

But let our girls give themselves time, or let time be allowed them, to give a year or two to the real study of languages, not in the threadbare phrases of the tourist and motorist, nor to mere drawing-room small talk; not with "matriculation standard" as an object, but to read the best that has been written, and try to speak according to the best that can be said now, and to write according to the standard of what is really excellent to-day; then the study of modern languages is lifted quite on to another plane. The particular advantage of this plane is that there is a view from it, wider in proportion to the number of languages known and to the grasp that is acquired of each, and the particular educational gift to be found there is width of sympathy and understanding. Defective sympathies, national and racial prejudices thrive upon a lower level. The *elect* of all nations understand one another, and are strangely alike; the lower we go down in the various grades of each nation the more is the divergency accentuated between one and another. Corresponding to this is mutual understanding through language; the better we possess the language of any nation the closer touch we can acquire with all that is theirs, with their best.

A superficial knowledge of languages rather accentuates than removes limitations, multiplies mistakes and embitters them. With a half-knowledge we misunderstand each other's ideals, we lose the point of the best things that are said, we fail to catch the aroma of the spices and the spirit of the living word; in fact, we are mere tourists in each other's mental world, and what word could better express the attitude of mind of one who is a stranger, but not a pilgrim, a tramp of a rather more civilized kind, having neither ties nor sympathies nor obligations, nothing to give, and more inclined to take than to receive. To create ties, sympathies, and obligations in the mental life, is a grace belonging to the study of languages, and makes it possible to give and receive hospitality on the best terms with the minds of those of other nations than our own. This is particularly a gift for the education of girls, since all graces of hospitality ought to be peculiarly theirs. To lift them above prejudices, to make them love other beauties than those of their own mental kindred, to afford them a wider possibility of giving happiness to others, and of making themselves at home in many countries, is to give them a power over the conditions of life which reaches very far into their own mental well-being and that of others, and makes them in the best meaning of the word cosmopolitan.

The choice of languages to be learnt must depend upon many considerations, but the widest good for English girls, though not the most easy to attain, is to give them perfect French. German is easier to learn from its kinship with our own language, but its grammar is of less educational value than French, and it does not help as French does to the acquirement of the most attractive of other European languages.

As a second language, however, and for a great deal that is not otherwise attainable, German is in general the best that can be chosen. Italian and Spanish have their special claims, but at present in England their appeal is not to the many. German gives the feeling of kindred minds near to us, ourselves yet not ourselves; with primitive Teutonic strength and directness, with a sweet freshness of spring in its more delicate poetry, and both of these elements blended at times in an atmosphere as of German forests in June. In some writers the flicker of French brilliancy illumines the depth of these Teutonic woods, producing a German which, in spite of the condemnation of the Emperor, we should like to write ourselves if the choice were offered to us.

But, notwithstanding the depth and strength of German, it is generally agreed that as an instrument of thought French prose in a master-hand is unrivalled, by its subtlety and precision, and its epigrammatic force. Every one knows and laments the decadent style which is eating into it; and every one knows that the deplorable tone of much of its contemporary literature makes discernment in French reading a matter not only of education but of conscience and sanity; but this does not make the danger to be inherent in the French language; obliging translators are ready to furnish us, in our own language and according to taste, with the very worst taken, from everywhere. And these faults do not affect the beauty of the instrument, nor its marvellous aptitude for training the mind to precision of expression. The logical bent of the French mind, its love of rule, the elaborateness of its conventions in literature, its ceremonial observances dating from by-gone times, the custom of giving account of everything, of letting no nuance pass unchallenged or uncommented, have given it a power of expression and definiteness which holds together as a complete code of written and unwritten laws, and makes a perfect instrument of its kind. But the very completeness of it has seemed to some writers a fetter, and when they revolt against and break through it, their extravagance passes beyond all ordinary bounds. French represents the two extremes, unheard-of goodness, unequalled perfection, or indescribable badness and unrestraint. Unfortunately the unrestraint is making its way, and as with ourselves in England, the magazine literature in France grows more and more undesirable.

Yet there is unlimited room for reading, and for Catholics a great choice of what is excellent. The modern manner of writing the lives of the Saints has been very successfully cultivated of late years in

France, making them living human beings "interesting as fiction," to use an accepted standard of measurement, more appealingly credible and more imitable than those older works in which they walked remote from the life of to-day, angelic rather than human. There are studies in criticism, too, and essays in practical psychology and social science, which bring within the scope of ordinary readers a great deal which with us can only be reached over rough roads and by-ways. No doubt each method has its advantages; the laboriously acquired knowledge becomes more completely a part of ourselves, but along the metalled way it is obvious that we cover more ground.

The comparison of these values leads to the practical question of translations. The Italian saying which identifies the translator with the traitor ought to give way to a more grateful and hopeful modern recognition of the services done by conscientious translations. We have undoubtedly suffered in England in the past by well-meaning but incompetent translators, especially of spiritual books, who have given us such impressions as to mislead us about the minds of the writers or even turned us against them altogether, to our own great loss. But at present more care is exercised, and conscientious critical exactitude in translating important spiritual works has given us English versions that are not unworthy of their originals. [1--An example of this is the late Canon Mackey's edition of the complete works of St. Francis of Sales, which has, unfortunately, to be completed without him.]

There is good service to be done to the Church in England by this work of translation, and it is one in which grown-up girls, if they have been sufficiently trained, might give valuable help. It must be borne in mind that not every book which is beautiful or useful in its own language, is desirable to translate. Some depend so much upon the genius of the language and the mentality of their native country that they simply evaporate in translation; others appeal so markedly to national points of view that they seem anomalous in other languages, as a good deal of our present-day English writing would appear in French. It has also to be impressed on translators that their responsibility is great; that it takes laborious persistence to make a really good translation, doing justice to both sides, giving the spirit of the author as well as his literal meaning, and not straining the language of the translation into unnatural forms to make it carry a sense that it does not easily bear.

The beauty of a translator's work is in the perfect accord of conscience and freedom, and this is not attained without unwearied search for the right word, the only right word which will give the true meaning and the true expression of any idea. To believe that this right word exists is one of the delights of translating; to be a lover of choice and beautiful words is an attraction in itself, leading to the love of things more beautiful still, the love of truth, and fitness, and transparency; the exercise of thought, and discrimination, and balance, and especially of a quality most rare and precious in women--mental patience. It is said that we excel in moral patience, but that when we approach anything intellectual this enduring virtue disappears, and we must "reach the goal in a bound or never arrive there at all." The sustained search for the perfect word would do much to correct this impatience, and if the search is aided by a knowledge of several modern languages so that comparative meanings and uses may be balanced against one another, it will be found not only to open rich veins of thought, but to give an ever-increasing power of working the mines and extracting the gold.

CHAPTER X.

HISTORY.

"We have heard, O God, with our ears: our fathers have declared to us, 'The work thou hast wrought in their days, and in the days of old.'"--Psalm XLIII.

"Thus independent of times and places, the Popes have never found any difficulty, when the proper moment came, of following out a new and daring line of policy (as their astonished foes have called it), of leaving the old world to shift for itself and to disappear from the scene in its due season, and of fastening on and establishing themselves in the new.

"I am led to this line of thought by St. Gregory's behaviour to the Anglo-Saxon race, on the break-up of the old civilisation."--Cardinal Newman, "Historical Sketches," III, "A Characteristic of the

Popes."

Of the so-called secular subjects history is the one
which depends most for its value upon the honour
in which it is held and upon the standpoint from
which it is taught. Not that history can be truly a
secular subject if it is taught as a whole--isolated
periods 01 subdivisions may be separated from the
rest and studied in a purely secular spirit, or with no
spirit at all--for the animating principle is not in the
subdivided parts but in the whole, and only if it is
taught as a whole can it receive the honour which
belongs to it as the "study of kings," the school of
experience and judgment, and one of the greatest
teachers of truth.

In modern times, since the fall of the Western
Empire, European history has centred, whether for
love or for hatred, round the Church; and it is thus
that Catholic education comes to its own in this
study, and the Catholic mind is more at home
among the phenomena and problems of history than
other minds for whom the ages of faith are only
vaults of superstition, or periods of mental
servitude, or at best, ages of high romance. Without
the Church what are the ideals of the Crusades, of
the Holy Roman Empire, of the religious spirit of
chivalry, or the struggle concerning Investitures, the
temporal power of the Popes and their temporal
sovereignty, the misery of the "Babylonian
Captivity," the development of the religious orders-
-in contemporary history--the Italian question
during the last fifty years, or the present position of
the Church in France? These are incomprehensible
phenomena without the Church to give the key to

the controversies and meaning to the ideals. Without knowing the Catholic Church from within, it is impossible to conceive of all these things as realities affecting conscience and the purpose and direction of life; their significance is lost if they have to be explained as the mere human struggle for supremacy of persons or classes, mere ecclesiastical disputes, or dreams of imperialism in Church matters. Take away the Church and try to draw up a course of lessons satisfactory to the minds even of girls under eighteen, and at every turn a thoughtful question may be critical, and the explanations in the hands of a non-Catholic teacher scarcely less futile than the efforts of old Kaspar to satisfy "young Peterkin" about the battle of Blenheim.

What about Investitures?

"Now tell us all about the war, And what they fought each other for?"

What about Canossa?

"What they fought each other for, I could not well make out. But everybody said" quoth he, "That 'twas a famous victory."

What about Mentana or Castel-Fidardo? "What good came of it at last?" Quoth little Peterkin. "Why that I cannot tell," said he, "But 'twas a famous victory."

The difficulty is tacitly acknowledged by the rare appearance of European history in the curriculum for non-Catholic girls' schools. But in any school

where the studies are set to meet the requirements
of examinations, the teaching of history is of
necessity dethroned from the place which belongs
to it by right. History deserves a position that is
central and commanding, a scheme that is
impressive when seen as a whole in retrospect, it
deserves to be taught from a point of view which
has not to be reconsidered in later years, and this is
to be found with all the stability possible, and with
every facility for later extension in the natural
arrangement of all modern history round the history
of the Church.

During the great development which has taken
place in the study of history within the last century,
and especially within the last fifty years, the mass of
materials has grown so enormous and the list of
authors of eminence so imposing that one might
almost despair of adapting the subject in any way to
a child's world if it were not for this central point of
view, in which the Incarnation and the Church are
the controlling facts dominating all others and
giving them their due place and proportion. On this
commanding point of observation the child and the
historian may stand side by side, each seeing truth
according to their capacity, and if the child should
grow into a historian it would be with an unbroken
development--there would not be anything to
unlearn. The method of "concentric" teaching
against which there is so much to be said when
applied to national history or to other branches of
teaching is entirely appropriate here, because no
wider vision of the world can be attained than from
the point whence the Church views it, in her
warfare to make the kingdoms of the world become

the kingdom of God and His Christ that He may reign for ever and ever. The Church beholds the *rational* not the *sensible* horizon of history, and standing at her point of view, the great ones and the little ones of the earth, historians and children, can look at the same heavens, one with the scientific instruments of his observatory, the other with the naked eye of a child's faith and understanding.

But the teaching of history as it has been carried on for some years, would have to travel a long way to arrive at this central point of view. As an educational subject a great deal has been done to destroy its value, by what was intended to give it assistance and stimulus. The history syllabus and requirements for University Local and other examinations have produced specially adapted text-books, in which facts and summaries have been arranged in order with wonderful care and forethought, to "meet all requirements"; but the kind intention with which every possible need has been foreseen between the covers of one text-book has defeated its own purpose, the living thing is no longer there--its skeleton remains, and after handling the dry bones and putting them in order and giving an account of them to the examining body, the children escape with relief to something more real, to the people of fiction who, however impossible to believe in, are at least flesh and blood, and have some points of contact with their own lives. "Of course as we go up for examinations here," wrote a child from a new school, "we only learn the summaries and genealogies of history and other subjects." A sidelight on the fruit of such a plan is often cast in the appreciations of its pupils.

"Did you like history?" "No I hated it, I can't bear names and dates." "What did you think of so and so?" "He wasn't in my period." So history has become names and dates, genealogies and summaries, hard pebbles instead of bread. It is unfair to children thus to prejudice them against a subject which thrills with human interest, and touches human life at every turn, it is unfair to history to present it thus, it is misleading to give development to a particular period without any general scheme against which it may show in due proportion, as misleading as the old picture-books for children in which the bat on one page and the man on the other were of the same size.

There must necessarily be a principle of selection, but one of the elements to be considered in making choice ought always to be that of proportion and of fitness in adaptation to a general scheme. It was pointed out by Sir Joshua Fitch in his "Lessons on Teaching" (an old-fashioned book now, since it was published before the deluge of "Pedagogics," but still valuable) that an ideal plan of teaching history to children might be found in the historical books of Holy Scripture, and in practice the idea is useful, suggesting that one aim should be kept in view, that at times the guiding line should contract to a mere clue of direction, and at others expand into very full and vivid narrative chiefly in biographical form. The principle may be applied in the teaching of any history that may be given to children, that is to say, in general, to Sacred history which has its own place in connexion with religious teaching, to ancient history within very small limits, to Greek and Roman history in such proportion as the years of education may allow, and to the two most prominent and most necessary for children, the history of their own country and that of modern Europe directed along the lines of the history of the Church.

There are periods and degrees of development in the minds of children to which correspond different manners of teaching and even different objects, as we make appeal to one or other of the growing faculties. The first stage is imaginative, the second calls not only upon the imagination and memory but upon the understanding, and the third, which is the beginning of a period of fruition, begins to exercise the judgment, and to give some ideas concerning principles of research and criticism.

The first is the period of romance, when by means of the best myths of many nations, from their heroic legends and later stories, the minds of children are turned to what is high and beautiful in the traditions of the past, and they learn those truths concerning human life and destiny which transcend the more limited truths of literal records of fact. In the beginning they are, to children, only stories, but we know ourselves that we can never exhaust the value of what came to us through the story of the wanderings of Ulysses, or the mysterious beauty of the Northern and Western myths, as the story of Balder or the children of Lir. The art of telling stories is beginning to be taught with wonderful power and beauty, the storyteller is turning into the pioneer of the historian, coming in advance to occupy the land, so that history may have "staked out a claim" before the examining bodies can arrive, in the dry season, to tread down the young growth.

The second period makes appeal to the intelligence, as well as to the imagination, and to this stage belongs particularly the study of the national history, the history of their own race and country; for English girls the history of England, not yet constitutional history, but the history of the Constitution with that of the kings and people, and further the history of the Empire. To this period of education belong the great lessons of loyalty and patriotism, that piety towards our own country which is so much on the decline as the home tie grows feebler. We do not want to teach the narrow patriotism which only finds expression in antagonism to and disparagement of other countries, but that which is shown by self-denial and self-sacrifice for the good of our own. The time to teach it is in that unsettled "middle age" of childhood when its exuberant feeling is in search of an ideal, when large moral effects can be appreciated, when there is some opening understanding of the value of character.

If the first period of childhood delights in what is strange, this second period gives its allegiance to what is strong, by preference to primitive and simple strength, to uncomplex aims and marked characters; it appreciates courage and endurance, and can bear to hear of sufferings which daunt the fastidiousness of those who are a few years older; perhaps it can endure so much because it realizes so little, but the fact remains true. This age exults in the sufferings of the martyrs and cannot bear the suggestion that plain duties may be heroic before

God. There is a great deal that may be done for minds in this period of development by the teaching of history if it is not crippled in its programme. To make concrete their ideals of greatness in the right personalities--a work which is as easily spoiled by a word out of season as a fine porcelain vase is cracked in a furnace--to direct their ideas of the aims of life towards worthy and unselfish ends, to foster true loyalty because of God from whom all authority comes--and this lesson has its pathetic poignancy for us in the history of our English martyrs--to show the claims that our country has upon the devotion of its sons and daughters, and to inspire some feeling of responsibility for its honour, especially to show the supreme worth of character and self-sacrifice, all these things may and must be taught in this middle period of children's education if they are to have any strong hold upon them in after life. It is a stubborn age in which teaching has to be on strong lines and deep ones; when the evolution of character is in the critical period that is to make or mar its future, it needs a strong hand over it, with power both to control and to support, a strong mind to command its respect, strong convictions to impress it, and strong principles on which to test its own young strength; and all those who have the privilege of teaching history to children of this age have an incomparable opportunity of training mind and character. The strength of our own convictions, the brightness of our own ideals, the fibre of our patriotism and loyalty will tell in the measure of two endowments, our own spirit of self-sacrifice and our tact. Children will detect the least false note if self-sacrifice is preached without experimental knowledge; and as it is the most contradictory of all ages, it takes every resource of tact to pilot it through channels for which there is no chart. The masterpieces of educators are wrought in this difficult but most interesting material.

Those who come after them will see what they have done, they cannot see it themselves. With less difficulty perhaps, because reason is more developed and the hot-headed and irritable phase of character is passing away, they will be able to apply the principles which have been laid down. With less difficulty, that is to say against less resistance, but not with less responsibility or even with less anxiety. For the nearer the work approaches to its completion and the more perfectly it has been begun, the more deeply must anyone approaching to lay hand upon it feel the need for great reverence, and self-restraint, and patience, and vigilance, not to spoil by careless interference that which is ready to receive and to give all that is best in youth, not to be unworthy of the confidence which a young mind is willing to place in its guidance.

For although so much stress is laid upon the impressionability of first childhood and the ineffaceable marks that are engraven on it, yet as to all that belongs to the mind and judgment this third period, in the early years of adolescence, is more sensitive still, because real criticism is just beginning to be possible and appreciation is in its spring-tide, now for the first time fully alive and awake. A transition line has been passed, and the study of history, like everything else, enters upon a new phase. The elementary teaching which has been sufficient up to this, which has in fact been the only possible teaching, must widen out in the third period, and the relative importance of aims is the line on which the change to more advanced teaching is felt.

The exercise of judgment becomes the chief object, and to direct this aright is the principal duty of those who teach at this age. It is not easy to give a right discernment and true views. To begin with one must have them oneself, and be able to support them with facts and arguments, they must have the weight of patient work behind them, and have settled themselves deeply in the mind; opinions freshly gathered that very day from an article or an essay are attractive and interesting and they appeal very strongly to young minds looking out for theories and clues, but they only give superficial help; in general, essay-writers and journalists do not expect to be taken too seriously, they intend to be suggestive rather than convincing, and it is a great matter to have the principle understood by girls, that it is not to the journalists that they must look for the last word in a controversy, nor for a permanent presentment of contemporary history. Again, it is necessary to remember the waywardness of girls' minds, and that it is conviction, not submission of views that we must aim at. A show of authority is out of place, the tone that "you must think as I do," tends without any bad will on the part of children to exasperate them and rouse the spirit of opposition, whereas a patient and even deferential hearing of their views and admission of their difficulties ensures at least a mind free from irritation and impatience, to listen and to take into

account what we have to say. They are not to be
blamed for having difficulties in accepting what we
put before them; on the contrary we must welcome
their independent thought even if it seems
aggressive and conceited; their positive assurance
that they see to the end of things is characteristic of
their age, but it is better that they should show
themselves thus, than through want of thought or
courage fall in with everything that is set before
them, or, worse still, take that pose of impartiality
which allows no views at all, and in the end
obliterates the line between right and wrong. The
too submissive minds which give no trouble now,
are laying it all up for the future. They accept what
we tell them without opposition, others will come
later on, telling them something different, and they
will accept it in the same way, and correct their
views day by day to the readings of the daily paper,
or of the *vogue* of their own particular set. These
are the minds which in the end are absorbed by the
world: the Church receives neither love nor service
from them.

Judgment may be passed upon actions as right or
wrong in themselves, or as practically adapting
means to end; the first is of great interest even to
young children, but for them it is all black or white,
and characters are to them entirely good or entirely
bad, deserving of unmixed admiration or of their
most excellent hatred, which they pour out simply
and vehemently, rejoicing without qualms of pity
when punishment overtakes the wrongdoer and
retributive justice is done to the wicked. This is
perhaps what makes them seem bloodthirsty in their
vengeance; they feel that so it ought to be, and that

the affirmation of principle is of more account than the individual. They detest half-measures and compromise. For the elder girls it is not so simple, and the nearer they come to our own times the more necessary is it to put before them that good is not always unaccompanied by evil nor evil by good.

In the last two or three years of a girl's education all the time that can be spared may be most profitably spent on the study of modern history, since it is there that the more complex problems are found, and there also that they will understand how contemporary questions have their springs in the past, and see the rise of the forces which are at work now, disintegrating the nations of Europe and shaking the foundations of every government. There are grave lessons to be learnt, not in gloomy or threatening forecasts but in showing the direction of cause and effect and the renewal of the same struggle which has been from the beginning, in ever fresh phases. The outcome of historical teaching to Catholics can never be discouragement or depression, whatever the forecast. The past gives confidence, and, when the glories of bygone ages are weighed against their troubles, and the Church's troubles now against her inward strength and her new horizons of hope, there is great reason for gratitude that we live in our own much-abused time. In every age the Church has, with her roots in the past, some buds and blossoms in the present and some fruit coming on for the future. Hailstorms may cut off both blossoms and fruit, but all will not be lost. We can always hold up our heads; there are buds on the fig-tree and we know in whom we have believed.

In bringing home to children these grounds for thankfulness, the quality of one's own mind and views tells very strongly, and this leads to the consideration of what is chiefly required in teaching history to children, and to girls growing up. The first and most essential point is that we ourselves should care about what we teach, not that we should merely like history as a school subject, but that it should be real to us, that we should feel something about it, joy or triumph or indignation, things which are not found in text-books, and we should believe that it all matters very much to the children and to ourselves. Lessons of the text-book type, facts, dates, summaries, and synopses matter very little to children, but people are of great importance, and if they grasp what often they only half believe, that what they are repeating as a mere lesson really took place among people who saw and felt it as vividly as they would themselves, then their sympathies and understanding are carried beyond the bounds of their school-rooms and respond to the touch of the great doings and sufferings of the race.

It is above all in the history of the Church that this sympathetic understanding becomes real. The interest of olden times in secular history is more dramatic and picturesque than real to children; but in the history of the Church and especially of the personalities of the popes the continuity of her life is very keenly felt; the popes are all of to-day, they transcend the boundaries of their times because in a number of ways they did and had to do and bear the very same things that are done and have to be borne by the popes of our own day. If we give to girls some vivid realization, say, of the troubled

Pontificate of Boniface VIII, with the violence and tragedy and pathos in which it ended, after the dust and jarring and weariness of battle in which it was spent; if they have entered into something of the anguish of Pius VII, they will more fully understand and feel deeper love and sympathy for the living, suffering successor now in the same chair, in another phase of the same conflict, with the Gentiles and peoples of the rising democracies taking counsel together against him, as kings and rulers did in the past, all imagining the same "vain thing," that they can overcome Christ and His Vicar.

Besides this living sympathy with what we teach, we must be able to speak truth without being afraid of its consequences. There was at one time a fear in the minds of Catholic teachers that by admitting that any of the popes had been unworthy of their charge, or that there had ever been abuses which called for reforms among clergy and religious and Catholic laity, they would be giving away the case for the Church and imperilling the faith and loyalty of children; that it was better they should only hear these things later, with the hope that they would never hear them at all. The real peril is in the course thus adopted. Surrounded as we are by non-Catholics, and in a time when no Catholic escapes from questions and attacks, open or covert, upon what we believe, the greatest injustice to the girls themselves, and to the honour of the faith, was to send them out unarmed against what they must necessarily meet. The first challenge would be met with a flat denial of facts, loyal-heartedly and confidently given; then would come a suspicion that there might be something in it, the inquiry which would show that this was really the case; then a certain right indignation, "Why was I not told the truth?" and a sense of insecurity vaguely disturbing the foundations which ought to be on immovable bed-rock. At the best, such an experience produces what builders call a "settlement," not dangerous to the fabric but unsightly in its consequences; it may, however, go much further, first to shake and then to loosen the whole spiritual building by the insinuation of doubt everywhere. It is impossible to forewarn children against all the charges which they may hear against the Church, but two points well established in their minds will give them confidence.

1. That the evidence which is brought to light year after year from access to State papers and documents tells on the side of the Church, as we say in England, of "the old religion," and not against it. Books by non-Catholics are more convincing than others in this matter, since they are free from the suspicion of partisanship; for instance, Gairdner's "Lollardy and the Reformation" which disposes of many mythical monsters of Protestant history.

2. That even if the facts were still more authentic to justify personal attacks on some of the popes, even if the abuses in the Church had not been grossly exaggerated, even putting facts at their worst, granting all that is assumed, it tends to strengthen faith rather than to undermine it, for the existence of the Church and the Papacy as they are to-day is a wonder only enhanced by every proof that it ought to have perished long ago according to all human

probability. With that confidence and assurance
even our little girls may hold their heads high, with
their faith and trust in the Church quite unabashed,
and wait for an answer if they cannot give it to
others or to themselves at the moment. "We have no
occasion to answer thee concerning this matter,"
said the three holy children to Nabuchodonosor, and
so may our own children say if they are hard
pressed, "your charges do but confirm our faith, we
have no occasion to answer."

It is impossible to leave so great a subject as history
without saying a word on the manner of teaching it
(for in this a manner is needed rather than a
method), when it is emancipated from the fetters of
prescribed periods and programmes which attach it
entirely to text-books. Text-books are not useless
but they are very hard to find, and many Catholic
text-books, much to be desired, are still unwritten,
especially in England. America has made more
effort in this direction than we. But the strength of
historical teaching for children and girls at school
lies in oral lessons, and of these it would seem that
the most effective form is not the conversational
lesson which is so valuable in other subjects, nor
the formal lesson with "steps," but the form of a
story for little ones; for older children the narrative
leading up to a point of view, with conversational
intervals, and encouragement for thoughtful
questions, especially at the end of the lesson; and in
the last years an informal kind of lecture, a
transition from school-room methods to the style of
formal lectures which maybe attended later.

Lessons in history are often spoiled by futile

questions put in as it were for conscience' sake, to satisfy the obligation of questioning, or to rouse the flagging attention of a child, but this is too great a sacrifice. It is artistically a fault to jar the whole movement of a good narrative for the sake of running after one truant mind. It is also artistically wrong and jarring to go abruptly from the climax of a story, or narrative, or lecture which has stirred some deep thought or emotion, and call with a sudden change of tone for recapitulation, or summary, or discussion. Silence is best; the greater lessons of history ought to transcend the limits of mere lessons, they are part of life, and they tell more upon the mind if they are dissociated from the harness and trappings of school work. Written papers for younger students and essays for seniors are the best means of calling for their results, and of guiding the line of reading by which all oral teaching of history and study of text-books must be supplemented.

When school-room education is finished what we may look for is that girls should be ready and inclined to take up some further study of history, by private reading or following lectures with intelligence, and that they should be able to express themselves clearly in writing, either in the form of notes, papers, or essays, so as to give an account of their work and their opinions to those who may direct these later studies. We may hope that what they have learned of European history will enable them to travel with understanding and appreciation, that places with a history will mean something to them, and that the great impression of a living past may set a deep mark upon them with its discipline of proportion that makes them personally so small and yet so great, small in proportion to all that has been, great in their inheritance from the whole past and in expectation of all that is yet to be.

CHAPTER XI.

ART.

"Give honour unto Luke Evangelist: For he it was (the aged legends say) Who first taught Art to fold her hands and pray. Scarcely at once she dared to rend the mist Of devious symbols: but soon having wist How sky-breadth and field-silence and this day Are symbols also in some deeper way, She looked through these to God, and was God's priest.

"And if, past noon, her toil began to irk, And she sought talismans, and turned in vain To soulless self-reflections of man's skill, Yet now, in this the twilight, she might still Kneel in the latter grass to pray again, Ere the night cometh and she may not work." DANTE GABRIEL ROSSETTI.

When we consider how much of the direction of life depends upon the quality of our taste, upon right discernment in what we like and dislike, it is evident that few things can be more important in education than to direct this directing force, and both to learn and teach the taste for what is best as far as possible in all things. For in the matter of taste nothing is unimportant. Taste influences us in every department of life, as our tastes are, so are we. The whole quality of our inner and outer life takes its tone from the things in which we find pleasure, from our standard of taste. If we are severe in our requirements, hard to please, and at least honest with ourselves, it will mean that a spur of continual dissatisfaction pricks us, in all we do, into habitual striving for an excellence which remains beyond our reach. But on the other hand we shall have to guard against that peevish fastidiousness which narrows itself down until it can see nothing but defects and faults, and loses the power of humbly and genuinely admiring. This passive dissatisfaction which attempts nothing of its own, and only finds fault with what is done by others, grows very fast if it is allowed to take hold, and produces a mental habit of merely destructive criticism or perpetual scolding. Safe in attempting nothing itself, unassailable and self-righteous as a Pharisee, this spirit can only pull down but not build up again. In children it is often the outcome of a little jealousy and want of personal courage; they can be helped to overcome it, but if it is allowed to grow up, dissatisfaction allied to pusillanimity are very difficult to correct.

On the other hand, if we are amiably and cheerfully inclined to admire things in general in a popular way, easily pleased and not exacting, we shall both receive and give a great deal of pleasure, but it will be all in a second and third and fourth-rate order of delight, and although this comfortable turn of mind is saved from much that is painful and jarring, it is not exempt from the danger of itself jarring continually upon the feelings of others, of pandering to the downward tendency in what is popular, and, in education, of debasing the standard of taste and discrimination for children. To be swayed by popularity in matters of taste is to accept mediocrity wholesale. We have left too far behind the ages when the taste of the people could give sound and true judgment in matters of art; we have left them at a distance which can be measured by what lies between the greatest Greek tragedies and contemporary popular plays. Consternation is frequently expressed at seeing how theatres of every grade are crowded with children of all classes in life, so it is from these popular plays that they must be learning the first lessons of dramatic criticism.

There are only rare instances of taste which is instinctively true, and the process of educational pressure tends to level down original thought in children, as the excess of magazine and newspaper reading works in the same direction for older minds, so that true, independent taste becomes more rare; the result does not seem favourable to the development of the best discernment in those who ought to sway the taste of their generation. If taste in art is entirely guided by that of others, and especially by fashion, it cannot attain to the possession of an independent point of view; yet this in a modest degree every one with some training might aspire to. But under the sway of fashion taste is cowed; it becomes conventional, and falls under the dominion of the current price of works of art. On the other hand it is more unfortunate to be self-taught in matters of taste than in any other order of things. In this point taste ranks with manners, which are, after all, a department of the same region of right feeling and discernment. If taste is untaught and spontaneous, it is generally unreliable and without consistency. If self-taught it can hardly help becoming dogmatic and oracular, as some highly gifted minds have become, making themselves the supreme court of appeal for their own day.

But trained taste is grounded in reverence and discipleship, a lowly and firm basis for departure, from which it may, if it has the power to do or to discern, rise in its strength, and leave behind those who have shown the way, or soar in great flights beyond their view. So it has often been seen in the history of art, and such is the right order of growth. It needs the living voice and the attentive mind, the influence of trained and experienced judgment to guide us in the beginning, but the guide must let us go at last and we must rely upon ourselves.

The bad effect of being either self-taught or conventional is exclusiveness; in one case the personal bias is too marked, in the other the temporary aspect appeals too strongly. In the education of taste it is needful that the child should "eat butter and honey," not only so as to refuse the evil and choose the good, but also to judge between good and good, and to know butter from honey and honey from butter. This is the principal end of the study of art in early education. The *doing* is very elementary, but the principles of discernment are something for life, feeding the springs of choice and delight, and making sure that they shall run clear and untroubled.

Teaching concerning art which can be given to girls has to be approached with a sense of responsibility from conviction of the importance of its bearing on character as a whole. Let anyone who has tried it pass in review a number of girls as they grow up, and judge whether their instinct in art does not give a key to their character, always supposing that they have some inclination to reflect on matters of beauty, for there are some who are candidly indifferent to beauty if they can have excitement. They have probably been spoiled as children and find it hard to recover. Excitement has worn the senses so that their report grows dull and feeble. Imagination runs on other lines and requires stimulants; there is no stillness of mind in which the perception of beauty and harmony and fitness can grow up.

There are others--may they be few--in whose minds there is little room for anything but success. Utilitarians in social life, their determination is to get on, and this spirit pervades all they do; it has the making of the hardest-grained worldliness: to these art has nothing to say. But there are others to whom it has a definite message, and their response to it corresponds to various schools or stages of art. There are some who are daring and explicit in their taste; they resent the curb, and rush into what is extravagant with a very feeble protest against it from within themselves. Beside them are simpler minds, merely exuberant, for whom there can never be enough light or colour in their picture of life. If they are gifted with enough intelligence to steady their joyful constitution of mind, these will often develop a taste that is fine and true. In the background of the group are generally a few silent members of sensitive temperament and deeper intuition, who see with marvellous quickness, but see too much to be happy and content, almost too much to be true. They incline towards another extreme, an ideal so high-pitched as to become unreal, and it meets with the penalty of unreality in over-balancing itself. Children nearly always pull to one side or the other; it is a work of long patience even to make them accept that there should be a golden mean. Did they ever need it so much as they do now? Probably each generation in turn, from Solomon's time onward, has asked the same question. But in the modern world there can hardly have been a time in which the principle of moderation needed to be more sustained, for there has never been a time when circumstances made man more daring in face of the forces of nature, and this same daring in other directions, less beautiful, is apt to become defiant and unashamed of excess. It asserts itself most loudly in modern French art, but we are following close behind, less logical and with more remaining traditions of correctness, but influenced beyond what we like to own.

In the education of girls, which is subject to so many limitations, very often short in itself, always too short for what would be desirable to attain, the best way to harmonize aesthetic teaching is not to treat it in different departments, but to centre all round the general history of art. This leaves in every stage the possibility of taking up particular branches of art study, whether historical, or technical, or practical, and these will find their right place, not dissociated from their antecedents and causes, not paramount but subordinate, and thus rightly proportioned and true in their relation to the whole progress of mankind in striving after beauty and the expression of it.

The history of art in connexion with the general history of the human race is a complement to it, ministering to the understanding of what is most intimate, stamping the expression of the dominant emotion on the countenance of every succeeding age. This is what its art has left to us, a more confidential record than its annals and chronicles, and more accessible to the young, who can often understand feelings before they can take account of facts in their historical importance. In any case the facts are clothed in living forms there where belief and aspiration and feeling have expressed themselves in works of art. If we value for children the whole impression of the centuries, especially in European history, more than the mere record of changes, the history of art will allow them to apprehend it almost as the biographies of great persons who have set their signature upon the age in which they lived.

As each of the fine arts has its own history which moves along divergent or parallel lines in different countries and periods, and as each development or check is bound up with the history of the country or period and bears its impress, the interpretation of one is assisted and enriched by the other, and both are linked together to illuminate the truth. It is only necessary to consider the position of Christian art in the thirteenth and fourteenth centuries, and the changes wrought by the Renaissance, to estimate the value of some knowledge of it in giving to children a right understanding of those times and of what they have left to the world. Again, the inferences to be drawn from the varied developments of Gothic architecture in France, Spain, and England are roads indicated to what is possible to explore in later studies, both in history and in art. And so the schools of painting studied in their history make ready the way for closer study in after years. Pugin's "Book of Contrasts" is an illustration full of suggestive power as to the service which may be rendered in teaching by comparing the art of one century with that of another, as expressive of the spirit of each period, and a means of reading below the surface.

Without Pugin's bitterness the same method of contrast has been used most effectively to put before children by means of lantern slides and lectures the manner in which art renders truth according to the various ideals and convictions of the artists. It is a lesson in itself, a lesson in faith, in devotion, as well as in art and in the history of man's mind, to show in succession, or even side by side, though the shock is painful, works of art in which the Christian mysteries are rendered in an age of faith or in one of unbelief. They can see in the great works of Catholic art how faith exults in setting them forth, with undoubting assurance, with a theological grasp of their bearings and conclusions, with plenitude of conviction and devotion that has no afterthoughts; and in contrasting with these the strained efforts to represent the same subjects without the illumination of theology they will learn to measure the distance downwards in art from faith to unbelief.

The conclusions may carry them further, to judge from the most modern paintings of the tone of mind of their own time, of its impatience and restlessness and want of hope. Let them compare the patient finish, the complete thought given to every detail in the works of the greatest painters, the accumulated light and depth, the abounding life, with the hasty, jagged, contemporary manner of painting, straining into harshness from want of patience, tense and angular from want of real vitality, exhausted from the absence of inward repose. They will comment for themselves upon the pessimism to which so many surrender themselves, taking with them their religious art, with its feeble Madonnas and haggard saints, without hope or courage or help, painted out of the abundance of their own heart's sadness. This contrast carries much teaching to the children of to-day if they can understand it, for each one who sets value upon faith and hope and resolution and courage in art is a unit adding strength to the line of defence against the invasions of sadness and dejection of spirit.

These considerations belong to the moral and spiritual value of the study of art, in the early years of an education intended to be general. They are of primary importance although in themselves only indirect results of the study. As to its direct results, it may be said in general that two things must be aimed at during the years of school life, appreciation of the beautiful in the whole realm of art, and some very elementary execution in one or other branch, some doing or making according to the gift of each one.

The work on both sides is and can be only preparation, only the establishment of principles and the laying of foundations; if anything further is attempted during school life it is apt to throw the rest of the education out of proportion, for in nothing whatever can a girl leaving the school-room be looked upon as having finished. It is a great deal if she is well-grounded and ready to begin. Even the very branches of study to which a disproportioned space has been allowed will suffer the penalty of it later on, for the narrow basis of incomplete foundations tends to make an ill-balanced superstructure which cannot bear the stress of effort required for perfection without falling into eccentricity or wearing itself out. Both misfortunes have been seen before now when infant prodigies have been allowed to grow on one side only. Restraint and control and general building up tend to strengthen even the talent which has apparently to be checked, by giving it space and equilibrium and the power of repose. Even if art should be their profession or their life-work in any form, the sacrifices made for general education will be compensated in the mental and moral balance of their work.

If general principles of art have been kept before the minds of children, and the history of art has given them some true ideas of its evolution, they are ready to learn the technique and practice of any branch to which they may be attracted. But as music and painting are more within their reach than other arts, it is reasonable that they should be provided for in the education of every child, so that each should have at least the offer and invitation of an entrance into those worlds, and latent talents be given the opportunity of declaring themselves. Poetry has its place apart, or rather it has two places, its own in the field of literature, and another, as an inspiration pervading all the domain of the fine arts, allied with music by a natural affinity, connected with painting on the side of imagination, related in one way or another to all that is expressive of the beautiful. Children will feel its influence before they can account for it, and it is well that they should do so--to feel it is in the direction of refusing the evil and choosing the good.

Music is coming into a more important place among educational influences now that the old superstition of making every child play the piano is passing away. It was an injustice both to the right reason of a child and to the honour of music when it was forced upon those who were unwilling and unfit to attain any degree of excellence in it. We are renouncing these superstitions and turning to something more widely possible--to cultivate the audience and teach them to listen with intelligence to that which without instruction is scarcely more than pleasant noise, or at best the expression of emotion. The intellectual aspect of music is beginning to be brought forward in teaching children, and with this awakening the whole effect of music in education is indefinitely raised. It has scarcely had time to tell yet, but as it extends more widely and makes its way through the whole of our educational system it may be hoped that the old complaints, too well founded, against the indifference and carelessness of English audiences, will be heard no more. We shall never attain to the kind of religious awe which falls upon a German audience, or to its moods of emotion, but we may reach some means of expression which the national character does not forbid, showing at least that we understand, even though we must not admit that we feel.

It is impossible to suggest what may be attained by girls of exceptional talent, but in practice if the average child-students, with fair musical ability, can at the end of their school course read and sing at sight fairly easy music, and have a good beginning of intelligent playing on one or two instruments, they will have brought their foundations in musical practice up to the level of their general education. If with some help they can understand the structure of a great musical work, and perhaps by themselves analyse an easy sonata, they will be in a position to appreciate the best of what they will hear afterwards, and if they have learnt something of the history of music and of the works of the great composers, their musical education will have gone as far as proportion allows before they are grown up. Some notions of harmony, enough to harmonize by the most elementary methods a simple melody, will be of the greatest service to those whose music has any future in it.

Catholic girls have a right and even a duty to learn something of the Church's own music; and in this also there are two things to be learnt--appreciation and execution. And amongst the practical applications of the art of music to life there is nothing more honourable than the acquired knowledge of ecclesiastical music to be used in the service of the Church. When the love and understanding of its spirit are acquired the diffusion of a right tone in Church music is a means of doing good, as true and as much within the reach of many girls as the spread of good literature; and in a small and indirect way it allows them the privilege of ministering to the beauty of Catholic worship and devotion.

The scope of drawing and painting in early education has been most ably treated of in many general and special works, and does not concern us here except in so far as it is connected with the training of taste in art which is of more importance to Catholics than to others, as has been considered above, in its relation to the springs of spiritual life, to faith and devotion, and also in so far as taste in art serves to strengthen or to undermine the principles on which conduct is based. We have to brace our children's wills to face restraint, to know that they cannot cast themselves at random and adrift in the pursuit of art, that their ideals must be more severe than those of others, and that they have less excuse than others if they allow these ideals to be debased. They ought to learn to be proud of this restraint, not to believe themselves thwarted or feel themselves galled by it, but to understand that it stands for a higher freedom by the side of which ease and unrestraint are more like servitude than liberty; it stands for the power to refuse the evil and choose the good; it stands for intellectual and moral freedom of choice, holding in check the impulse and inclination that are prompted from within and invited from without to escape from control.

The best teaching in this is to show what is best, and to give the principles by which it is to be judged. To talk of what is bad, or less good, even by way of warning, is less persuasive and calculated even to do harm to girls whose temper of mind is often "quite contrary." Warnings are wearisome to them, and when they refer to remote dangers, partly guessed at, mostly unknown, they even excite the spirit of adventure to go and find out for themselves, just as in childhood repeated warnings and threats of the nursery-maids and maiden aunts are the very things which set the spirit of enterprise off on the voyage of discovery, a fact which the head nurse and the mother have found out long ago, and so have learnt to refrain from these attractive advertisements of danger. So it is with teachers. We learn by experience that a trumpet blast of warning wakes the echoes at first and rouses all that is to be roused, but also that if it is often repeated it dulls the ear and calls forth no response at all. Quiet positive teaching convinces children; to show them the best things attracts them, and once their true allegiance is given to the best, they have more security within themselves than in many danger signals set up for their safety. What is most persuasive of all is a whole-hearted love for real truth and beauty in those who teach them. Their own glow of enthusiasm is caught, light from light, and taste from taste, and ideal from ideal; warning may be lost sight of, but this is living spirit and will last.

What children can accomplish by the excellent
methods of teaching drawing and painting which
are coming into use now, it is difficult to say. Talent
as well as circumstances and conditions of
education differ very widely in this. But as
preparation for intelligent appreciation they should
acquire some elementary principles of criticism, and
some knowledge of the history and of the different
schools of painting, indications of what to look for
here and there in Europe and likewise of how to
look at it; this is what they can take with them as a
foundation, and in some degree all can acquire
enough to continue their own education according
to their opportunities. Matter-of-fact minds can
learn enough not to be intolerable, the average
enough to guide and safeguard their taste. They are
important, for they will be in general the multitude,
the public, whose judgment is of consequence by its
weight of numbers; they will by their demand make
art go upwards or downwards according to their
pleasure. For the few, the precious few who are
chosen and gifted to have a more definite influence,
all the love they can acquire in their early years for
the best in art will attach them for life to what is
sane and true and lovely and of good fame.

The foundations of all this lie very deep in human
nature, and taste will be consistent with itself
throughout the whole of life. It manifests itself in
early sensitiveness and responsiveness to artistic
beauty. It determines the choice in what to love as
well as what to like. It will assert itself in
friendship, and estrangement in matters of taste is
often the first indication of a divergence in ideals
which continues and grows more marked until at

some crossroads one takes the higher path and the other the lower and their ways never meet again. That higher path, the disinterested love of beauty, calls for much sacrifice; it must seek its pleasure on ly in the highest, and not look for a first taste of delight, but a second, when the power of criticism has been schooled by a kind of asceticism to detect the choice from the vulgar and the true from the insincere. This spirit of sacrifice must enter into every form of training for life, but above all into the training of the Catholic mind. It has a wide range and asks much of its disciples, a certain renunciation and self-restraint in all things which never completely lets itself go. Catholic art bears witness to this: "Where a man seeks himself there he falls from love," says a Kempis, and this is proved not only in the love of God, but in what makes the glory of Christian art, the love of beauty and truth in the service of faith.

CHAPTER XII.

MANNERS.

"Manners are the happy ways of doing things; each-
-once--a stroke of genius or of love, now repeated
and hardened into usage."--EMERSON.

The late Queen Victoria had a profound sense of the
importance of manners and of certain
conventionalities, and the singular gift of common
sense, which stood for so much in her, stands also
for the significance of those things on which she
laid so much stress.

Conventionality has a bad name at present, and
manners are on the decline, this is a fact quite
undisputed. As to conventionalities it is assumed
that they represent an artificial and hollow code,
from the pressure of which all, and especially the
young, should be emancipated. And it may well be
that there is something to be said in favour of
modifying them--in fact it must be so, for all human
things need at times to be revised and readapted to
special and local conditions. To attempt to enforce
the same code of conventions on human society in
different countries, or at different stages of
development, is necessarily artificial, and if pressed
too far it provokes reaction, and in reaction we
almost inevitably go to extreme lengths. So in
reaction against too rigid conventionalities and a
social ritual which was perhaps over-exacting, we
are swinging out beyond control in the direction of
complete spontaneity. And yet there is need for a
code of conventions--for some established defence

against the instincts of selfishness which find their way back by a short cut to barbarism if they are not kept in check.

Civilized selfishness leads to a worse kind of barbarism than that of rude and primitive states of society, because it has more resources at its command, as cruelty with refinement has more resources for inflicting pain than cruelty which can only strike hard. Civilized selfishness is worse also in that it has let go of better things; it is not in progress towards a higher plane of life, but has turned its back upon ideals and is slipping on the down-grade without a check. We can see the complete expression of life without conventions in the unrestraint of "hooliganism" with us, and its equivalents in other countries. In this we observe the characteristic product of bringing up without either religion, or conventions, or teaching in good manners which are inseparable from religion. We see the demoralization of the very forces which make both the strength and the weakness of youth and a great part of its charm, the impetuosity, the fearlessness of consequence, the lightheartedness, the exuberance which would have been so strong for good if rightly turned, become through want of this right impetus and control not strong but violent, uncontrollable and reckless to a degree which terrifies the very authorities who are responsible for them, in that system which is bringing up children with nothing to hold by, and nothing to which they can appeal. Girls are inclined to go even further than boys in this unrestraint through their greater excitability and recklessness, and their having less instinct of self-preservation. It is a problem for the local authorities. Their lavish expenditure upon sanitation, adornment, and--to use the favourite word--"equipment" of their schools does not seem to touch it; in fact it cannot reach the real difficulty, for it makes appeal to the senses and neglects the soul, and the souls of children are hungry for faith and love and something higher to look for, beyond the well-being of to-day in the schools, and the struggle for life, in the streets, to-morrow.

It is not only in the elementary schools that such types of formidable selfishness are produced. In any class of life, in school or home, wherever a child is growing up without control and "handling," without the discipline of religion and manners, without the yoke of obligations enforcing respect and consideration for others, there a rough is being brought up, not so loud-voiced or so uncouth as the street-rough, but as much out of tune with goodness and honour, with as little to hold by and appeal to, as troublesome and dangerous either at home or in society, as uncertain and unreliable in a party or a ministry, and in any association that makes demand upon self-control in the name of duty.

This is very generally recognized and deplored, but except within the Church, which has kept the key to these questions, the remedy is hard to find. Inspectors of elementary schools have been heard to say that, even in districts where the Catholic school was composed of the poorest and roughest elements, the manners were better than those of the well-to-do children in the neighbouring Council schools. They could not account for it, but we can; the precious hour of religious teaching for which we have had to fight so hard, influences the whole day and helps to create the "Catholic atmosphere" which in its own way tells perhaps more widely than the teaching. Faith tells of the presence of God and this underlies the rest, while the sense of friendly protection, the love of Our Lady, the angels, and saints, the love of the priest who administers all that Catholic children most value, who blesses and absolves them in God's name, all these carry them out of what is wretched and depressing in their surroundings to a different world in which they give and receive love and respect as children of God. No wonder their manners are gentler and their intercourse more disposed to friendliness, there is something to appeal to and uphold, something to love.

The Protestant Reformation breaking up these relations and all the ceremonial observance in which they found expression, necessarily produced deterioration of manners. As soon as anyone, especially a child, becomes--not rightly but aggressively--independent, argumentatively preoccupied in asserting that "I am as good as you are, and I can do without you"--he falls from the right proportion of things, becomes less instead of greater, because he stands alone, and from this to warfare against all order and control the step is short. So it has proved. The principles of Protestantism worked out to the principles of the Revolution, and to their natural outcome, seen at its worst in the Reign of Terror and the Commune of 1871 in Paris.

Again the influence of the Church on manners was

dominant in the age of chivalry. At that time religion and manners were known to be inseparable, and it was the Church that handled the rough vigour of her sons to make them gentle as knights. This is so well known that it needs no more than calling to mind, and, turning attention to the fact that all the handling was fundamental, it is handling that makes manners. Even the derivation of the word does not let us forget this--*manners* from *manieres*, from *manier*, from *main*, from *manus*, the touch of the human hand upon the art of living worthily in human society, without offence and without contention, with the gentleness of a race, the *gens*, that owns a common origin, the urbanity of those who have learned to dwell in a city "compact together," the respect of those who have some one to look to for approval and control, either above them in dignity, or beneath them in strength, and therefore to be considered with due reverence.

The handling began early in days of chivalry, no time was lost, because there would necessarily be checks on the way. Knighthood was far off, but it could not be caught sight of too early as an ideal, and it was characteristic of the consideration of the Church that, in the scheme of manners over which she held sway, the first training of her knights was intrusted to women. For women set the standard of manners in every age, if a child has not learnt by seven years old how to behave towards them it is scarcely possible for him to learn it at all, and it is by women only that it can be taught. The little *damoiseaux* would have perfect and accomplished manners for their age when they left the apartments of the ladies at seven years old; it was a matter of course that they would fall off a good deal in their next stage. They would become "pert," as pages were supposed to be, and diffident as esquires, but as knights they would come back of themselves to the perfect ways of their childhood with a grace that became well the strength and self-possession of their knighthood. We have no longer the same formal and ceremonial training; it is not possible in our own times under the altered conditions of life, yet it commands attention for those who have at heart the future well-being of the boys and girls of to-day. The fundamental facts upon which manners are grounded remain the same. These are, some of them, worth consideration:--

1. That manners represent a great deal more than mere social observances; they stand as the outward expression of some of the deepest springs of conduct, and none of the modern magic of philanthropy-- altruism, culture, the freedom and good-fellowship of democracy, replaces them, because, in their spirit, manners belong to religion.

2. That manners are a matter of individual training, so that they could never be learnt from a book. They can scarcely be taught, except in their simplest elements, to a class or school as a whole, but the authority which stands nearest in responsibility to each child, either in the home circle or at school, has to make a special study of it in order to teach it manners. The reason of this is evident. In each nature selfishness crops out on one side rather than another, and it is this which has to be studied, that the forward may be repressed, the shy or indolent stimulated, the dreamy quickened into attention,

and all the other defective sides recognized and taken, literally, *in hand*, to be modelled to a better form.

3. That training in manners is not a short course but a long course of study, a work of patience on both sides, of gentle and most insistent handling on one side and of long endurance on the other. There are a very few exquisite natures with whom the grace of manners seems to be inborn. They are not very vigorous, not physically robust; their own sensitiveness serves as a private tutor or monitor to tell them at the right moment what others feel, and what they should say or do. They have a great gift, but they lay down their price for it, and suffer for others as well as in themselves more than their share. But in general, the average boy and girl needs a "daily exercise" which in most cases amounts to "nagging," and in the best hands is only saved from nagging by its absence of peevishness, and the patience with which it reminds and urges and teases into perfect observance. The teasing thing, and yet the most necessary one, is the constant check upon the preoccupying interests of children, so that in presence of their elders they can never completely let themselves go, but have to be attentive to every service of consideration or mark of respect that occasion calls for. It is very wearisome, but when it has been acquired through laborious years--there it is, like a special sense superadded to the ordinary endowments of nature, giving presence of mind and self-possession, arming the whole being against surprise or awkwardness or indiscretion, and controlling what has so long appeared to exercise control over it--the conditions of social intercourse.

How shall we persuade the children of to-day that manners and conventions have not come to an end as part of the old regime which appears to them an elaborate unreality V It is exceedingly difficult to do so, at school especially, as in many cases their whole family consents to regard them as extinct, and only when startled at the over-growth of their girls' unmannerly roughness and self-assertion they send them to school "to have their manners attended to"; but then it is too late. The only way to form manners is to teach them from the beginning as a part of religion, as indeed they are. Devotion to Our Lady will give to the manners both of boys and girls something which stamps them as Christian and Catholic, something above the world's level. And, as has been so often pointed out, the Church's ritual is the court ceremonial of the most perfect manners, in which every least detail has its significance, and applies some principle of inward faith and devotion to outward service.

If we could get to the root of all that the older codes of manners required, and even the conventionalities of modern life--these remnants, in so far as they are based on the older codes--it would be found that, as in the Church's ceremonial, not one of them was without its meaning, but that all represented some principle of Christian conduct, even if they have developed into expressions which seem trivial. Human things tend to exaggeration and to "sport," as gardeners say, from their type into strange varieties, and so the manners which were the outcome of chivalry--exquisite, idealized, and restrained in their best period, grew artificial in later times and elaborated themselves into an etiquette which grew tyrannical and even ridiculous, and added violence to the inevitable reaction which followed. But if we look beyond the outward form to the spirit of such prescriptions as are left in force, there is something noble in their origin, either the laws of hospitality regulating all the relations of host and guest, or reverence for innocence and weakness which surrounded the dignity of both with lines of chivalrous defence, or the sensitiveness of personal honour, the instinct of what was due to oneself, an inward law that compelled a line of conduct that was unselfish and honourable. So the relics of these lofty conventions are deserving of all respect, and they cannot be disregarded without tampering with foundations which it is not safe to touch. They are falling into disrepute, but for the love of the children let us maintain them as far as we can. The experience of past ages has laid up lessons for us, and if we can take them in let us do so, if only as a training for children in self-control, for which they will find other uses a few years hence.

But in doing this we must take account of all that has changed. There are some antique forms, beautiful and full of dignity, which it is useless to attempt to revive; they cannot live again, they are too massive for our mobile manner of life to-day. And on the other hand there are some which are too high-pitched, or too delicate. We are living in a democratic age, and must be able to stand against its stress. So in the education of girls a greater measure of independence must necessarily be given to them, and they must learn to use it, to become self-reliant and self-protecting. They have to grow more conscious, less trustful, a little harder in outline; one kind of young dignity has to be exchanged for another, an attitude of self-defence is necessary. There is perhaps a certain loss in it, but it is inevitable. The real misfortune is that the first line of defence is often surrendered before the second is ready, and a sudden relaxation of control tends to yield too much; in fact girls are apt to lose their heads and abandon their self-control further than they are able to resume it. Once they have "let themselves go"--it is the favourite phrase, and for once a phrase that completely conveys its meaning-- it is exceedingly difficult for them to stop themselves, impossible for others to stop them by force, for the daring ones are quite ready to break with their friends, and the others can elude control with very little difficulty. The only security is a complete armour of self-control based on faith, and a home tie which is a guarantee for happiness. Girls who are not happy in their own homes live in an atmosphere of temptation which they can scarcely resist, and the happiness of home is dependent in a great measure upon the manners of home, "there is no surer dissolvant of home affections than discourtesy." [1--D. Urquhart.] It is useless to insist on this, it is known and admitted by almost all, but the remedy or the preventive is hard to apply, demanding such constant self-sacrifice on the part of parents that all are not ready to practise it; it is so much easier and it looks at first sight so kind to let children have their way. So kind at first, so unselfish in appearance, the parents giving way, abdicating their authority, while the young democracy in the nursery or school-room takes the reins in hand so willingly, makes the laws, or rather rules without them, by its sovereign moods, and then outgrows the "establishment" altogether, requires more scope, snaps the link with home, scarcely regretting, and goes off on its own account to elbow its way in the world. It is obviously necessary and perhaps desirable that many girls should have to make their own way in the world who would formerly have lived at home, but often the way in which it is done is all wrong, and leaves behind on both sides recollections with a touch of soreness.

For those who are practically concerned with the education of girls the question is how to attain what we want for them, while the force of the current is set so strongly against us. We have to make up our minds as to what conventions can survive and fix in some way the high and low-water marks, for there must be both, the highest that we can attain, and the lowest that we can accept. All material is not alike; some cannot take polish at all. It is well if it can be made tolerable; if it does not fall below that level of manners which are at least the safeguard of conduct; if it can impose upon itself and accept at least so much restraint as to make it inoffensive, not aggressively selfish. Perhaps the low-water mark might be fixed at the remembrance that other people have rights and the observance of their claims. This would secure at least the common marks of respect and the necessary conventionalities of intercourse. For ordinary use the high-water mark might attain to the remembrance that other people have feelings, and to taking them into account, and as an ordinary guide of conduct this includes a great deal and requires training and watchfulness to establish it, even where there is no exceptional selfishness or bluntness of sense to be overcome. The nature of an ordinary healthy energetic child, high-spirited and boisterous, full of a hundred interests of its own, finds the mere attention to these things a heavy yoke, and the constant self-denial needed to carry them out is a laborious work indeed.

The slow process of polishing marble has more than one point of resemblance with the training of manners; it is satisfactory to think that the resemblance goes further than the process, that as only by polishing can the concealed beauties of the marble be brought out, so only in the perfecting of manners will the finer grain of character and feeling be revealed. Polishing is a process which may reach different degrees of brilliancy according to the material on which it is performed; and so in the teaching of manners a great deal depends upon the quality of the nature, and the amount of expression which it is capable of acquiring. It is useless to press for what cannot be given, at the same time it is unfair not to exact the best that every one is able to give. As in all that has to do with character, example is better than precept.

But in the matter of manners example alone is by no means enough; precept is formally necessary, and precept has to be enforced by exercise. It is necessary because the origin of established conventionalities is remote; they do not speak for themselves, they are the outcome of a general habit of thought, they have come into being through a long succession of precedents. We cannot explain them fully to children; they can only have the summary and results of them, and these are dry and grinding, opposed to the unpremeditated spontaneous ways of acting in which they delight. Manners are almost fatally opposed to the sudden happy thoughts of doing something original, which occur to children's minds. No wonder they dislike them; we must be prepared for this. They are almost grown up before they can understand the value of what they have gone through in acquiring these habits of unselfishness, but unlike many other subjects to which they are obliged to give time and labour, they will not leave this behind in the schoolroom. It is then that they will begin to exercise with ease and precision of long practice the art of the best and most expressive conduct in every situation which their circumstances may create.

In connexion with this question of circumstances in life and the situations which arise out of them, there is one thing which ought to be taught to children as a fundamental principle, and that is the relation of manners to class of life, and what is meant by vulgarity. For vulgarity is not--what it is too often assumed to be--a matter of class, but in itself a matter of insincerity, the effort to appear or to be something that one is not. The contrary of vulgarity, by the word, is preciousness or distinction, and in conduct or act it is the perfect preciousness and distinction of truthfulness. Truthfulness in manners gives distinction and dignity in all classes of society; truthfulness gives that simplicity of manners which is one of the special graces of royalty, and also of an unspoiled and especially a Catholic peasantry. Vulgarity has an element of restless unreality and pretentious striving, an affectation or assumption of ways which do not belong to it, and in particular an unwillingness to serve, and a dread of owning any obligation of service. Yet service perfects manners and dignity, from the highest to the lowest, and the manners of perfect servants either public or private are models of dignity and fitness. The manners of the best servants often put to shame those of their employers, for their self-possession and complete knowledge of what they are and ought to be raises them above the unquietness of those who have a suspicion that they are not quite what might be expected of them. It is on this uncertain ground that all the blunders of manners occur; when simplicity is lost disaster follows, with loss of dignity and self-respect, and pretentiousness forces its way through to claim the respect which it is conscious of not deserving.

Truth, then, is the foundation of distinction in manners for every class, and the manners of children are beautiful and perfect when simplicity bears witness to inward truthfulness and consideration for others, when it expresses modesty as to themselves and kindness of heart towards every one. It does not require much display or much ceremonial for their manners to be perfect according to the requirements of life at present; the ritual of society is a variable thing, sometimes very exacting, at others disposed to every concession, but these things do not vary--truth, modesty, reverence, kindness are of all times, and these are the bases of our teaching.

The personal contribution of those who teach, the

influence of their companionship is that which
establishes the standard, their patience is the
measure which determines the limits of attainment,
for it is only patience which makes a perfect work,
whether the attainment be high or low. It takes more
patience to bring poor material up to a presentable
standard than to direct the quick intuitions of those
who are more responsive; in one case efforts meet
with resistance, in the other, generally with
correspondence. But our own practice is for
ourselves the important thing, for the inward
standard is the point of departure, and our own
sincerity is a light as well as a rule, or rather it is a
rule because it is a light; it prevents the standard of
manners from being double, one for use and one for
ornament; it imposes respect to be observed with
children as well as exacted from them, and it keeps
up the consciousness that manners represent faith
and, in a sense, duty to God rather than to one's
neighbour.

This, too, belongs not to the fleeting things of social
observance but to the deep springs of conduct, and
its teaching may be summed up in one question. Is
not well-instructed devotion to Our Lady and the
understanding of the Church's ceremonies a school
of manners in which we may learn how human
intercourse may be carried on with the most perfect
external expressiveness? Is not all inattention of
mind to the courtesies of life, all roughness and
slovenliness, all crude unconventionality which is
proud of its self-assertion, a "falling from love" in
seeking self? Will not the instinct of devotion and
imitation teach within, all those things which must
otherwise be learned by painful reiteration from

without; the perpetual _give up, give way, give thanks, make a fitting answer, pause, think of others, don't get excited, wait, serve_, which require watchfulness and self-sacrifice?

Perhaps in the last year or two of education, when our best opportunities occur, some insight will be gained into the deeper meaning of all these things. It may then be understood that they are something more than arbitrary rules; there may come the understanding of what is beautiful in human intercourse, of the excellence of self-restraint, the loveliness of perfect service. If this can be seen it will tone down all that is too uncontrolled and make self-restraint acceptable, and will deal with the conventions of life as with symbols, poor and inarticulate indeed, but profoundly significant, of things as they ought to be.

CHAPTER XIII.

HIGHER EDUCATION OP WOMEN.

"In die Erd' isi's aufgenommen, Glucklich ist die
Form gefullt; Wird's auch schon zu Tage kommen,
Dass es Fleiss und Kunst vergilt? Wenn der Guss
misslang? Wenn die Form zersprang? Ach,
vielleicht, indem wir hoffen, Hat uns Unheil schon
getroffen." SCHILLER, "Das Lied von der Gloeke."

So far in these pages the education of girls has only
been considered up to the age of eighteen or so, that
is to the end of the ordinary school-room course. At
eighteen, some say that it is just time to go to
school, and others consider that it is more than time
to leave it. They look at life from different points of
view. Some are eager to experience everything for
themselves, and as early as possible to snatch at this
good thing, life, which is theirs, and make what
they can of it, believing that its only interest is in
what lies beyond the bounds of childhood and a life
of regulated studies; they want to begin to *live*.
Others feel that life is such a good thing that every
year of longer preparation fits them better to make
the most of its opportunities, and others again are
anxious--for a particular purpose, sometimes, and
very rarely for the disinterested love of it--to
undertake a course of more advanced studies and
take active part in the movement "for the higher
education of women." The first will advance as far
as possible the date of their coming out; the second
will delay it as long as they are allowed, to give
themselves in quiet to the studies and thought which
grow in value to them month by month; the third,

energetic and decided, buckle on their armour and enter themselves at universities for degrees or certificates according to the facilities offered.

There can be no doubt that important changes were necessary in the education of women. About the middle of the last century it had reached a condition of stagnation from the passing away of the old system of instruction before anything was ready to take its place. With very few exceptions, and those depended entirely on the families from which they carae, girls were scarcely educated at all. The old system had given them few things but these were of value; manners, languages, a little music and domestic training would include it all, with perhaps a few notions of "the use of the globes" and arithmetic. But when it dwindled into a book called "Hangnail's Questions," and manners declined into primness, and domestic training lost its vigour, then artificiality laid hold of it and lethargy followed, and there was no more education for "young ladies."

In a characteristically English way it was individual effort which came to change the face of things, and honour is due to the pioneers who went first, facing opposition and believing in the possibilities of better things. In some other countries the State would have taken the initiative and has done so, but we have our own ways of working out things, "l'aveugle et tatonnante infaillibilite de l'Angleterre," as some one has called it, in which the individual goes first, and makes trial of the land, and often experiences failure in the first attempts. From the closing years of the eighteenth century, when the "Vindication of the Rights of Women" was published by Mary Wollstonecraft, the question has been more or less in agitation. But in 1848, with the opening of Queen's College in London, it took its first decided step forward in the direction of provision for the higher education of women, and in literature it was much in the air. Tennyson's "Princess" came in 1847, and "Aurora Leigh" from Elizabeth Barrett Browning in 1851, and things moved onward with increasing rapidity until at one moment it seemed like a rush to new goldfields. One university after another has granted degrees to women or degree certificates in place of the degrees which were refused; women are resident students at some universities and at others present themselves on equal terms with men for examination. The way has been opened to them in some professions and in many spheres of activity from which they had been formerly excluded.

One advantage of the English mode of proceeding in these great questions is that the situation can be reconsidered from time to time without the discordant contentions which surround any proclamation of non-success in State concerns. We feel our way and try this and that, and readjust ourselves, and a great deal of experimental knowledge has been gained before any great interests or the prestige of the State have been involved. These questions which affect a whole people directly or indirectly require, for us at least, a great deal of experimenting before we know what suits us. We are not very amenable to systems, or theories, or ready-made schemes. And the phenomenon of tides is very marked in all that we undertake. There is a period of advance and then a pause and a period of decline, and after another pause the tide rises again. It may perhaps be accounted for in part by the very fact that we do so much for ourselves in England, and look askance at anything which curtails the freedom of our movements, when we are in earnest about a question; but this independence is rapidly diminishing under the more elaborate administration of recent years, and the increase of State control in education. Whatever may be the effect of this in the future, it seems as if there were at present a moment of reconsideration as to whether we have been quite on the right track in the pursuit of higher education for women, and a certain discontent with what has been achieved so far. There are at all events not many who are cordially pleased with the results. Some dissatisfaction is felt as to the position of the girl students in residence at the universities. They cannot share in any true sense in the life of the universities, but only exist on their outskirts, outside the tradition of the past, a modern growth tolerated rather than fostered or valued by the authorities. This creates a position scarcely enviable in itself, or likely to communicate that particular tone which is the gift of the oldest English universities to their sons. Some girl students have undoubtedly distinguished themselves, especially at Cambridge; in the line of studies they attained what they sought, but that particular gift of the university they could not attain. It is lamented that the number of really disinterested students attending Girton and Newnham is small; the same complaint is heard from the Halls for women at Oxford; there is a certain want of confidence as to the future and what it is all leading to. To women with a professional career before them the degree certificates are of value, but the course of studies itself and its mental effect is conceded by many to be disappointing. One reason may be that the characteristics of girls' work affect in a way the whole movement. They are very eager and impetuous students, but in general the staying power is short; an excessive energy is put out in one direction, then it flags, and a new beginning is made towards another quarter. So in this general movement there have been successive stages of activity.

The higher education movement has gone on its own course. The first pioneers had clear and noble ideals; Bedford College, the growth of Cheltenham, the beginnings of Newnham and Girton Colleges, the North of England Ladies' "Council of Education" represented them. Now that the movement has left the port and gone beyond what they foresaw, it has met the difficulties of the open sea.

Nursing was another sphere opened about the same time, to meet the urgent needs felt during the Crimean War; it was admirably planned out by Florence Nightingale, again a pioneer with loftiest ideals. There followed a rush for that opening; it has continued, and now the same complaint is made that it is an outlet for those whose lives are not to their liking at home, rather than those who are conscious of a special fitness for it or recognized as having the particular qualities which it calls for. And then came the development of a new variety among the unemployed of the wealthier classes, the "athletic girl." Not every one could aspire to be an athletic girl, it requires some means, and much time; but it is there, and it is part of the emancipation movement. The latest in the field are the movements towards organization of effort, association on the lines of the German *Frauenbund*, and the French *Mouvement Feministe*, and beside them, around them, with or without them, the Women's Suffrage Movement, militant or non-militant. These are of the rising tide, and each tide makes a difference to our coast-line, in some places the sea gains, in others the land, and so the thinkers, for and against, register their victories and defeats, and the face of things continues to change more and more rapidly.

It seems an ungracious task, unfair--perhaps it seems above all retrograde and ignorant--to express doubt and not to think hopefully of a cause in which so many lives have been spent with singular disinterestedness and self-devotion. Yet these adverse thoughts are in the air, not only amongst those who are unable to win in the race, but amongst those who have won, and also amongst those who look out upon it all with undistracted and unbiassed interest; older men, who look to the end and outcome of things, to the ultimate direction when the forces have adjusted themselves. Those who think of the next generation are not quite satisfied with what is being done for our girls or by them.

Catholics have been spurred hotly into the movement by those who are keenly anxious that we

should not be left behind, but should show
ourselves able to be with the best in all these things.
Perhaps at the stage which has been reached we
have more reason than others to be dissatisfied with
the results of success, since we are more beset than
others by the haunting question--_what then_? For
those who have to devote themselves to the cause of
Catholic education it is often and increasingly
necessary to win degrees or their equivalents, not
altogether for their own value, but as the key that
fits the lock, for the gates to the domain of
education are kept locked by the State. And so in
other spheres of Catholic usefulness the key may
become more and more necessary. But--may it be
suggested--in their own education, a degree for a
man and a degree for a girl mean very different
things, even if the degree is the same. For a girl it is
the certificate of a course of studies. For a man an
Oxford or Cambridge degree means atmosphere
unique in character, immemorial tradition,
association, all kinds of interests and subtle
influences out of the past, the impressiveness of
numbers, among which the individual shows in very
modest proportions indeed whatever may be his
gifts. The difference is that of two worlds. Bat even
at other universities the degree means more to a
man if it is anything beyond a mere gate-key. It is
his initial effort, after which comes the full stress of
his life's work. For a girl, except in the rarest cases,
it is either a gate-key or a final effort, either her
life's work takes a different turn, or she thinks she
has had enough. The line of common studies is
adapted for man's work and programme of life. It
has been made to fit woman's professional work,
but the fit is not perfect. It has a marked unfitness in

its adaptation for women to the real end of higher education, or university education, which is the perfecting of the individual mind, according to its kind, in surroundings favourable to its complete development.

Atmosphere is a most important element at all periods of education, and in the education of girls all-important, and an atmosphere for the higher education of girls has not yet been created in the universities. The girl students are few, their position is not unassailable, their aims not very well defined, and the thing which is above all required for the intellectual development of girls--quiet of mind--is not assured. It is obvious that there can never be great tradition and a past to look back to, unless there is a present, and a beginning, and a long period of growth. But everything for the future consists in having a noble beginning, however lowly, true foundations and clear aims, and this we have not yet secured. It seems almost as if we had begun at the wrong end, that the foundations of character were not made strong enough, before the intellectual superstructure began to be raised--and that this gives the sense of insecurity. An unusual strength of character would be required to lead the way in living worthily under such difficult circumstances as have been created, a great self-restraint to walk without swerving or losing the track, without the controlling machinery of university rules and traditions, without experience, at the most adventurous age of life, and except in preparation for professional work without the steadying power of definite duties and obligations. A few could do it, but not many, and those chosen

few would have found their way in any case. The
past bears witness to this.

But the past as a whole bears other testimony which
is worth considering here. Through every
vicissitude of women's education there have always
been the few who were exceptional in mental and
moral strength, and they have held on their way,
and achieved a great deal, and left behind them
names deserving of honour. Such were Maria
Gaetana Agnesi, who was invited by the Pope and
the university to lecture in mathematics at Bologna
(and declined the invitation to give herself to the
service of the poor), and Lucretia Helena Gomaro
Piscopia, who taught philosophy and theology! and
Laura Bassi who lectured in physics, and Clara von
Schur-man who became proficient in Greek,
Hebrew, Syriac, and Chaldaic in order to study
Scripture "with greater independence and
judgment," and the Pirk-heimer family of
Nuremberg, Caritas and Clara and others, whose
attainments were conspicuous in their day. But
there is something unfamiliar about all these names;
they do not belong so much to the history of the
world as to the curiosities of literature and learning.
The world has not felt their touch upon it; we
should scarcely miss them in the galleries of history
if their portraits were taken down.

The women who have been really great, whom we
could not spare out of their place in history, have
not been the student women or the remarkably
learned. The greatest women have taken their place
in the life of the world, not in its libraries; their
strength has been in their character, their mission

civilization in its widest and loftiest sense. They
have ruled not with the "Divine right of kings," but
with the Divine right of queens, which is quite a
different title, undisputed and secure to them, if
they do not abdicate it of themselves or drag it into
the field of controversy to be matched and measured
against the Divine or human rights of kings. "The
heaven of heavens is the Lord's, but the earth He
has given to the children of men," and to woman He
seems to have assigned the borderland between the
two, to fit the one for the other and weld the links.
Hers are the first steps in training the souls of
children, the nurseries of the kingdom of heaven
(the mothers of saints would fill a portrait gallery of
their own); hers the special missions of peace and
reconciliation and encouragement, the hidden germs
of such great enterprises as the Propagation of the
Faith, and the trust of such great devotions as that
of the Blessed Sacrament and the Sacred Heart to be
brought within the reach of the faithful. The names
of Matilda of Tuscany, of St. Catherine of Siena, of
Blessed Joan of Arc, of Isabella the Catholic, of St.
Theresa are representative, amongst others, of
women who have fulfilled public missions for the
service of the Church, and of Christian people, and
for the realization of religious ideals: true queens of
the borderland between both worlds. Others have
reigned in their own spheres, in families or
solitudes, or cloistered enclosures--as the two Saints
Elizabeth, Paula and Eustochium and all their group
of friends, the great Abbesses Hildegarde, Hilda,
Gertrude and others, and the chosen line of
foundresses of religious orders--these too have
ruled the borderland, and their influence, direct or
indirect, has all been in the same direction, for

pacification and not for strife, for high aspiration and heavenly-mindedness, for faith and hope and love and self-devotion, and all those things for want of which the world is sick to death.

But the kingdom of woman is on that borderland, and if she comes down to earth to claim its lowland provinces she exposes herself to lose both worlds, not securing real freedom or permanent equality in one, and losing hold of some of the highest prerogatives of the other. These may seem to be cloudy and visionary views, and this does not in any sense pretend to be a controversial defence of them, but only a suggestion that both history and present experience have something to say on this side of the question, a suggestion also that there are two spheres of influence, requiring different qualities for their perfect use, as there are two forces in a planetary system. If these forces attempted to work on one line the result would be the wreck of the whole, but in their balance one against the other, apparently contrary, in reality at one, the equilibrium of the whole is secured. One is for motor force and the other for central control; both working in concert establish the harmony of planetary motion and give permanent conditions of unity. Here, as elsewhere, uniformity tends to ultimate loosening of unity; diversity establishes that balance which combines freedom with stability.

Once more it must be said that only the Catholic Church can give perfect adjustment to the two forces, as she holds up on both sides ideals which make for unity. And when the higher education of women has flowered under Catholic influence, it has had a strong basis of moral worth, of discipline and control to sustain the expansion of intellectual life; and without the Church the higher education of women has tended to one-sidedness, to nonconformity of manners, of character, and of mind, to extremes, to want of balance, and to loss of equilibrium in the social order, by straining after uniformity of rights and aims and occupations.

So with regard to the general question of women's higher education may it be suggested that the moral training, the strengthening of character, is the side which must have precedence and must accompany every step of their education, making them fit to bear heavier responsibilities, to control their own larger independence, to stand against the current of disintegrating influences that will play upon them. To be fit for higher education calls for much acquired self-restraint, and unfortunately it is on the contrary sometimes sought as an opening for speedier emancipation from control. Those who seek it in this spirit are of all others least fitted to receive it, for the aim is false, and it gives a false movement to the whole being. Again, when it is entirely dissociated from the realities of life, it tends to unfit girls for any but a professional career in which they will have--at great cost to their own well-being--to renounce their contact with those primeval teachers of experience.

In some countries they have found means of combining both in a modified form of university life for girls, and in this they are wiser than we. Buds of the same tree have been introduced into England, but they are nipped by want of appreciation. We have still to look to our foundations, and even to make up our minds as to what we want. Perhaps the next few years will make things clearer. But in the meantime there is a great deal to be done; there is one lesson that every one concerned with girls must teach them, and induce them to learn, that is the lesson of self-command and decision. Our girls are in danger of drifting and floating along the current of the hour, passive in critical moments, wanting in perseverance to carry out anything that requires steady effort. They are often forced to walk upon slippery ground; temptations sometimes creep on insensibly, and at others make such sudden attacks that the thing all others to be dreaded for girls is want of courage and decision of character. Those render them the best service who train them early to decide for themselves, to say yes or no definitely, to make up their mind promptly, not because they "feel like it" but for a reason which they know, and to keep in the same mind which they have reasonably made up. Thus they may be fitted by higher moral education to receive higher mental training according to their gifts; but in any case they will be prepared by it to take up whatever responsibilities life may throw upon them.

The future of girls necessarily remains indeterminate, at least until the last years of their education, but the long indeterminate time is not lost if it has been spent in preparatory training of mind, and especially in giving some resistance to their pliant or wayward characters. Thus, whether they devote themselves to the well-being of their own families, or give themselves to volunteer work in any department, social or particular, or advance

in the direction of higher studies, or receive any
special call from God to dedicate their gifts to His
particular service, they will at least have something
to give; their education will have been "higher" in
that it has raised them above the dead level of
mediocre character and will-power, which is only
responsive to the inclination or stimulus of the
moment, but has no definite plan of life. It may be
that as far as exterior work goes, or anything that
has a name to it, no specified life-work will be
offered to many, but it is a pity if they regard their
lives as a failure on that account.

There are lives whose occupations could not be
expressed in a formula, yet they are precious to
their surroundings and precious in themselves,
requiring more steady self-sacrifice than those
which give the stimulus of something definite to do.
These need not feel themselves cut off from what is
highest in woman's education, if they realize that
the mind has a life in itself and makes its own
existence there, not selfishly, but indeed in a
peculiarly selfless way, because it has nothing to
show for itself but some small round of
unimpressive occupations; some perpetual call upon
its sympathies and devotion, not enough to fill a
life, but just enough to prevent it from turning to
anything else. Then the higher life has to be almost
entirely within itself, and no one is there to see the
value of it all, least of all the one who lives it. There
is no stimulus, no success, no brilliancy; it is
perhaps of all lives the hardest to accept, yet what
perfect workmanship it sometimes shows. Its
disappearance often reveals a whole tissue of
indirect influences which had gone forth from it;

and who can tell how far this unregistered, uncertificated higher education of a woman, without a degree and with an exceedingly unassuming opinion of itself, may have extended. It is a life hard to accept, difficult to put into words with any due proportion to its worth, but good and beautiful to know, surely "rich in the sight of God,"

CHAPTER XIV.

CONCLUSION.

"Far out the strange ships go: Their broad sails
flashing red As flame, or white as snow: The ships,
as David said. 'Winds rush and waters roll: Their
strength, their beauty, brings Into mine heart the
whole Magnificence of things.'" LIONEL
JOHNSON.

The conclusion is only an opportunity for repeating
how much there is still to be said, and even more to
be thought of and to be done, in the great problem
and work of educating girls. Every generation has to
face the same problem, and deals with it in a
characteristic way. For us it presents particular
features of interest, of hope and likewise of anxious
concern. The interest of education never flags; year
after year the material is new, the children come up
from the nursery to the school-room, with their life
before them, their unbounded possibilities for good,
their confidence and expectant hopefulness as to
what the future will bring them. We have our
splendid opportunity and are greatly responsible for
its use. Each precious result of education when the
girl has grown up and leaves our hands is thrown
into the furnace to be tried--fired--like glass or fine
porcelain. Those who educate have, at a given
moment, to let go of their control, and however
solicitously they may have foreseen and prepared
for it by gradually obliging children to act without
coercion and be responsible for themselves, yet the
critical moment must come at last and "every man's
work shall be manifest," "the fire shall try every

man's work, of what sort it is" (1 Cor. III). Life tries the work of education, "of what sort it is." If it stands the test it is more beautiful than before, its colours are fixed. If it breaks, and some will inevitably break in the trial, a Catholic education has left in the soul a way to recovery. Nothing, with us, is hopelessly shattered, we always know how to make things right again. But if we can we must secure the character against breaking, our effort in education must be to make something that will last, and for this we must often sacrifice present success in consideration of the future, we must not want to see results. A small finished building is a more sightly object than one which is only beginning to rise above its foundations, yet we should choose that our educational work should be like the second rather than the first, even though it has reached "the ugly stage," though it has its disappointments and troubles before it, with its daily risks and the uncertainty of ultimate success. But it is a truer work, and a better introduction to the realities of life.

A "finished education" is an illusion or else a lasting disappointment; the very word implies a condition of mind which is opposed to any further development, a condition of self-satisfaction. What then shall we call a well-educated girl, whom we consider ready for the opportunities and responsibilities of her new life? An equal degree of fitness cannot be expected from all, the difference between those who have ten talents and those who have only two will always be felt. Those who have less will be well educated if they have acquired spirit enough not to be discontented or disheartened at feeling that their resources are small; if we have been able to inspire them with hope and plodding patience it will be a great thing, for this unconquerable spirit of perseverance does not fail in the end, it attains to something worthy of all honour, it gives us people of trust whose character is equal to their responsibilities, and that is no little thing in any position of life; and, if to this steadiness of will is added a contented mind, it will always be superior to its circumstances and will not cease to develop in the line of its best qualities.

It is not these who disappoint--in fact they often give more than was expected of them. It is those of great promise who are more often disappointing in failing to realize what they might do with their richer endowments; they fail in strength of will.

Now if we want a girl to grow to the best that a woman ought to be it is in two things that we must establish her fundamentally--quiet of mind and firmness of will. Quiet of mind equally removed from stagnation and from excitement. In stagnation her mind is open to the seven evil spirits who came into the house that was empty and swept; under excitement it is carried to extremes in any direction which occupies its attention at the time. The best minds of women are quiet, intuitive, and full of intellectual sympathies. They are not in general made for initiation and creation, but initiation and creation lean upon them for understanding and support. And their support must be moral as well as mental, for this they need firmness of will. Support cannot be given to others without an inward support which does not fail towards itself in critical moments. The great victories of women have been won by this inward support, this firmness and perseverance of will based upon faith. The will of a woman is strong, not in the measure of what it manifests without, as of what it reserves within, that is to say in the moderation of its own impulsiveness and emotional tendency, in the self-discipline of perseverance, the subordination of personal interest to the good of whatever depends upon it for support. It is great in self-devotion, and in this is found its only lasting independence.

To give much and ask little in personal return is independence of the highest kind. But faith alone can make it possible. The Catholic Faith gives that particular orientation of mind which is independent of this world, knowing the account which it must give to God. To some it is duty and the reign of conscience, to others it is detachment and the reign of the love of God, the joyful flight of the soul towards heavenly things. The particular name matters little, it has a centre of gravity. "As everlasting foundations upon a solid rock, so the commandments of God in the heart of a holy woman." [1--Ecclus. XXVI. 24.]

APPENDIX I.

EXTRACT FROM "THE BLESSED
SACRAMENT" BY FATHER FABER.
BOOK III. SEC. VII.

Let us put aside the curtain of vindicative fire, and
see what this pain of loss is like; I say, what it is
like, for it fortunately surpasses human imagination
to conceive its dire reality. Suppose that we could
see the huge planets and the ponderous stars
whirling their terrific masses with awful, and if it
might be so, clamorous velocity, and thundering
through the fields of unresisting space with furious
gigantic momentum, such as the mighty avalanche
most feebly figures, and thus describing with
chafing eccentricities and frightful deflections, their
mighty centre-seeking and centre-flying circles, we
should behold in the nakedness of its tremendous
operations the Divine law of gravitation. Thus in
like manner should we see the true relations
between God and ourselves, the true meaning and
worth of His beneficent presence, if we could
behold a lost soul at the moment of its final and
judicial reprobation, a few moments after its
separation from the body and in all the strength of
its disembodied vigour and the fierceness of its
penal immortality.
No beast of the jungle, no chimera of heathen
imagination, could be so appalling. No sooner is the
impassable bar placed between God and itself than
what theologians call the creature's radical love of
the Creator breaks out in a perfect tempest of
undying efforts. It seeks its centre and it cannot
reach it. It bounds up towards God, and is dashed

down again. It thrusts and beats against the granite
walls of its prison with such incredible force, that
the planet must be strong indeed whose equilibrium
is not disturbed by the weight of that spiritual
violence. Yet the great law of gravitation is stronger
still, and the planet swings smoothly through its
beautiful ether. Nothing can madden the reason of
the disembodied soul, else the view of the
desirableness of God and the inefficacious
attractions of the glorious Divinity would do so.
Up and down its burning cage the many-facultied
and mightily intelligenced spirit wastes its
excruciating immortality in varying and ever
varying still, always beginning and monotonously
completing, like a caged beast upon its iron tether, a
threefold movement, which is not three movements
successively, but one triple movement all at once.
In rage it would fain get at God to seize Him,
dethrone Him, murder Him, and destroy Him; in
agony it would fain suffocate its own interior thirst
for God, which parches and burns it with all the
frantic horrors of a perfectly self-possessed frenzy;
and in fury it would fain break its tight fetters of
gnawing fire which pin down its radical love of the
beautiful Sovereign Good, and drag it ever back
with cruel wrench from its desperate propension to
its uncreated Centre. In the mingling of these three
efforts it lives its life of endless horrors. Portentous
as is the vehemence with which it shoots forth its
imprecations against God, they fall faint and
harmless, far short of His tranquil, song-surrounded
throne.
Pour views of its own hideous state revolve around
the lost soul, like the pictures of some ghastly show.
One while it sees the million times ten million

genera and species of pains of sense which meet
and form a loathsome union with this vast central
pain of loss. Another while all the multitude of
graces, the countless kind providences, which it has
wasted pass before it, and generate that undying
worm of remorse of which Our Saviour speaks.
Then comes a keen but joyless view, a calculation,
but only a bankrupt's calculation, of the possibility
of gains for ever forfeited, of all the grandeur and
ocean-like vastness of the bliss which it has lost.
Last of all comes before it the immensity of God, to
it so unconsoling and so unprofitable; it is not a
picture, it is only a formless shadow, yet it knows
instinctively that it is God. With a cry that should
be heard creation through, it rushes upon Him, and
it knocks itself, spirit as it is, against material
terrors. It clasps the shadow of God, and, lo! it
embraces keen flames. It runs up to Him but it has
encountered only fearful demons. It leaps the length
of its chain after Him, but it has only dashed into an
affrighting crowd of lost and cursed souls. Thus is it
ever writhing under the sense of being its own
executioner. Thus there is not an hour of our
summer sunshine, not a moment of our sweet
starlight, not a vibration of our moonlit groves, not
an undulation of odorous air from our flowerbeds,
not a pulse of delicious sound from music or song
to us, but that hapless unpitiable soul is ever falling
sick afresh of the overwhelming sense that all
around it is eternal.

EXTRACT FROM "THE CREATOR AND THE
CREATURE." BY FATHER FABER.
BOOK II. CH. V.

Yet the heavenly joys of the illuminated
understanding far transcend the thrills of the
glorified senses. The contemplation of heavenly
beauty and of heavenly truth must indeed be beyond
all our earthly standards of comparison. The
clearness and instantaneousness of all the mental
processes, the complete exclusion of error, the
unbroken serenity of the vision, the facility of
embracing whole worlds and systems in one calm,
searching, exhausting glance, the Divine character
and utter holiness of all the truths presented to the
view--these are broken words which serve at least
to show what we may even 'now indistinctly covet
in that bright abode of everlasting bliss. Intelligent
intercourse with the angelic choirs, and the
incessant transmission of the Divine splendours
through them to our minds, cannot be thought of
without our perceiving that the keen pleasures and
deep sensibilities of the intellectual world on earth
are but poor, thin, unsubstantial shadows of the
exulting immortal life of our glorified minds above.
The very expansion of the faculties of the soul, and
the probable disclosure in it of many new faculties
which have no object of exercise in this land of
exile, are in themselves pleasures which we can
hardly picture to ourselves. To be rescued from all
narrowness, and for ever; to possess at all times a
perfect consciousness of our whole undying selves,
and to possess and retain that self-consciousness in
the bright light of God; to feel the supernatural
corroborations of the light of glory, securing to us

powers of contemplation such as the highest
mystical theology can only faintly and feebly
imitate; to expatiate in God, delivered from the
monotony of human things; to be securely poised in
the highest flights of our immense capacities,
without any sense of weariness, or any chance of a
reaction; who can think out for himself the realities
of a life like this?

Yet what is all this compared with one hour, one of
earth's short hours, of the magnificences of celestial
love? Oh to turn our whole souls upon God, and
souls thus expanded and thus glorified; to have our
affections multiplied and magnified a thousandfold,
and then girded up and strengthened by immortality
to bear the beauty of God to be unveiled before us;
and even so strengthened, to be rapt by it into a
sublime amazement which has no similitude on
earth; to be carried away by the inebriating torrents
of love, and yet be firm in the most steadfast
adoration; to have passionate desire, yet without
tumult or disturbance; to have the most bewildering
intensity along with an unearthly calmness; to lose
ourselves in God, and then find ourselves there
more our own than ever; to love rapturously and to
be loved again still more rapturously, and then for
our love to grow more rapturous still, and again the
return of our love to be still outstripping what we
gave, and then for us to love even yet more and
more and more rapturously, and again, and again,
and again to have it so returned, and still the great
waters of God's love to flow over us and overwhelm
us until the vehemence of our impassioned peace
and the daring vigour of our yearning adoration
reach beyond the sight of our most venturous
imagining; what is all this but for our souls to live a

life of the most intelligent entrancing ecstasy, and yet not be shivered by the fiery heat? There have been times on earth when we have caught our own hearts loving God, and there was a flash of light, and then a tear, and after that we lay down to rest. O happy that we were! Worlds could not purchase from us even the memory of those moments. And yet when we think of heaven, we may own that we know not yet what manner of thing it is to love the Lord Our God.

APPENDIX II

From a Pastoral Letter of His Eminence Cardinal
Bourne, Archbishop of Westminster, written when
Bishop of Southwark. Quinquagesima Sunday,
1901.

...Every age has its own difficulties and dangers. At
the present day we are exposed to temptations
which at the beginning of the last century were of
comparatively small account. It will be so always.
Every new development of human activity, every
invention of human ingenuity, is meant by God to
serve to His honour, and to the good of His
creatures. We must accept them all gratefully as the
results of the intelligence which He has been
pleased to bestow upon us. At the same time the
experience of every age teaches us that the
weakness and perversity of many wrest to evil
purposes these gifts, which in the Divine intention
should serve only for good. It is against the
perverted use of two of God's gifts that we would
very earnestly warn you to-day.
During the last century the power that men have of
conveying their thoughts to others has been
multiplied incredibly by the facility of the printed
word. Thoughts uttered in speech or sermon were
given but to a few hundreds who came within the
reach of the human voice. Even when they were
communicated to manuscript they came to the
knowledge of very few. What a complete change
has now been wrought. In the shortest space of time
men's ideas are conveyed all over the world, and
they may become at once a power for good or for
evil in every place, and millions who have never

seen or heard him whose thoughts they read, are brought to some extent under his influence.

Again, at the present day all men read, more or less. The number of those who are unable to do so is rapidly diminishing, and a man who cannot read will soon be practically unknown. As a matter of fact men read a great deal, and they are very largely influenced by what they read.

Thus the multiplicity of printed matter, and the widespread power of reading have created a situation fraught with immense possibilities for good, but no less exposed to distinct occasions of evil and of sin. It is to such occasions of sin, dear children in Jesus Christ, that we desire to direct your attention this Lent.

Every gift of God brings with it responsibility on our part in the use that we make of it. The supreme gift of intelligence and free-will are powers to enable us to love and serve God, but we are able to use them to dishonour and outrage Him. So with all the other faculties that flow from these two great gifts. Beading and books have brought many souls nearer to their Creator. Many souls, on the other hand, have been ruined eternally by the books which they have read. It is dearly, therefore, of importance to us to know how to use wisely these gifts that we possess.

The Holy Catholic Church, the Guardian of God's Truth, and the unflinching upholder of the moral law, has been always alive to her duty in this matter, and from the earliest times has claimed and exercised the right of pointing out to her children books that are dangerous to faith or virtue. This is one of the duties of bishops, and, in a most special manner, of the Sacred Congregation of the Index.

And, though at the present day, owing to the decay of religious belief, this authority cannot be exercised in the same way as of old, it is on that very account all the more necessary for us to bear well in mind, and to carry out fully in practice, the great unchanging principles on which the legislation of the Church in this matter has been ever based. You are bound, dear children in Jesus Christ, to guard yourselves against all those things which may be a source of danger to your faith or purity of heart. You have no right to tamper with the one or the other. Therefore, in the first place, it is the duty of Catholics to abstain from reading all such books as are written directly with the object of attacking the Christian Faith, or undermining the foundations of morality. If men of learning and position are called upon to read such works in order to refute them, they must do so with the fear of God before their eyes. They must fortify themselves by prayer and spiritual reading, even as men protect themselves from contagion, where they have to enter a poisonous atmosphere. Mere curiosity, still less the desire to pass as well informed in every newest theory, will not suffice to justify us in exposing ourselves to so grave a risk.

Again, there are many books, especially works of fiction, in which false principles are often indirectly conveyed, and by which the imagination may be dangerously excited. With regard to such reading, it is very hard to give one definite rule, for its effect on different characters varies so much. A book most dangerous to one may be almost without harm to another, on account of the latter's want of vivid imagination. Again, a book full of danger to the youth or girl may be absolutely without effect on

one of maturer years. The one and only rule is to be
absolutely loyal and true to our conscience, and if
the voice of conscience is not sufficiently distinct,
to seek guidance and advice from those upon whom
we can rely, and above all, from the director of our
souls. If we take up a book, and we find that,
without foolish scruple, it is raising doubts in our
mind or exciting our imagination in perilous
directions, then we must be brave enough to close
it, and not open it again. If our weakness is such
that we cannot resist temptation, which unforeseen
may come upon us, then it is our duty not to read
any book the character of which is quite unknown
to us. If any such book is a source of temptation to
us, we must shun it, if we wish to do our duty to
God. If our reading makes us discontented with the
lot in life which Divine Providence has assigned to
us, if it leads us to neglect or do ill the duties of our
position, if we find that our trust in God is lessening
and our love of this world growing, in all these
cases we must examine ourselves with the greatest
care, and banish from ourselves any book which is
having these evil effects upon us.

Lastly there is an immense amount of literature,
mostly of an ephemeral character, which almost of
necessity enters very largely into our lives at the
present day. We cannot characterize it as wholly
bad, though its influence is not entirely good, but it
is hopeless to attempt to counteract what is harmful
in it by any direct means. The newspapers and
magazines of the hour are often without apparent
harm, and yet very often their arguments are based
on principles which are unsound, and their spirit is
frankly worldly, and entirely opposed to the
teaching of Jesus Christ and of the Gospel. Still

more when the Catholic Church and the Holy See are in question, we know full well, and the most recent experience has proved it, that they are often consciously or unconsciously untruthful. Even when their misrepresentations have been exposed, in spite of the boasted fairness of our country, we know that we must not always expect a withdrawal of false news, still less adequate apology. Constant reading of this character cannot but weaken the Catholic sense and instinct, and engender in their place a worldly and critical spirit most harmful in every way, unless we take means to counteract it. What are these means? A place must be found in your lives, dear children in Jesus Christ, for reading of a distinctly Catholic character. You must endeavour to know the actual life and doings of the Catholic Church at home and abroad by the reading of Catholic periodical literature. You must have at hand books of instruction in the Catholic Faith, for at least occasional reading, so as to keep alive in your minds the full teaching of the Church. You must give due place to strictly spiritual reading, such as the "Holy Gospels," "The Following of Christ," "The Introduction to a Devout Life" by St. Francis of Sales, and the lives of the Saints, which are now published in every form and at every price. It is not your duty to abstain from reading all the current literature of the day, but it is your duty to nourish your Catholic mental life by purely Catholic literature. The more you read of secular works, the more urgent is your duty to give a sufficient place to those also, which will directly serve you in doing your duty to God and in saving your soul. Assuredly one of the most pressing duties at the present day is to recognize fully our personal and individual responsibility in this matter of reading, and to examine our conscience closely to see how we are acquitting ourselves of it.

Before we leave this subject, we wish to ask all those among you dear children in Jesus Christ, who, whether as fathers and mothers, or as members of religious institutes, or masters and mistresses in schools, are charged with the education of the young, to do all in your power to train those committed to you to a wise and full understanding of this matter of reading, and to a realization of its enormous power for good and harm, and, therefore, to a sense of the extreme responsibility attaching to it. Make them understand that, while all are able to read, all things are not to be read by all; that this power, like every power, may be abused, and that we have to learn how to use it with due restraint. While they are with you and gladly subject to your influence, train their judgment and their taste in reading, so that they may know what is good and true, and know how to turn from what is evil and false. Such a trained and cultivated judgment is the best protection that you can bestow upon them. Some dangers must be overcome by flight, but there are far more, especially at the present day, which must be faced, and then overcome. It is part of your great vocation to prepare and equip these children to be brave and to conquer in this fight. Gradually, therefore, accustom them to the dangers they may meet in reading. Train their judgment, strengthen their wills, make them loyal to conscience, and then, trusting in God's grace, give them to their work in life.

Made in the USA
Middletown, DE
12 August 2024

58935806R10139